And Other Misadventures in God's Outdoors

Steven R. Gilliland

Author's Voice
McPherson, Kansas

A Coon in My Coveralls and Other Misadventures in God's Outdoors
By Steven R. Gilliland

Copyright © 2019 by Steven R. Gilliland
All rights reserved. No part of this book may be reproduced or transmitted in any form or by any means, electronic or mechanical, including photocopying, recording or by any information storage and retrieval system, without the written permission from the author, except for brief quotations in a review.

Illustrations (cover and interior) by Vernon Buller
Cover and interior design by Jan Gilbert Hurst

ISBN: 978-0-578-46429-9
Library of Congress Control Number: 2019916006

*I dedicate this book to God
for creating for us such an awesome playground,
and to an avid hunter, adventurer, and outdoorsman
—our late grandpa Hosafros,
who endowed this family with his outdoor spirit.
Without them this book would never have happened.*

Acknowledgments

Many thanks to Vernon Buller from Montezuma, Kansas, for all the cartoons. Vernon, you are the best cartoonist ever!

Sincere thanks to my wife Joyce for accompanying me on many ill-fated and sidesplitting adventures and for graciously allowing me to include her in many columns and stories.

Special thanks to Carol Shuetze and the staff at The Territorial Magazine for the privilege of writing for their wonderful publication and for allowing me to combine these stories into my book.

Thanks also to Jan Hurst, owner of Author's Voice, for her patience with me and for her wisdom in putting together my book.

Thanks to my little brother Joe and to my sisters Louann, Rose, and Sue, and to all my nieces, nephews, and cousins who keep the outdoor spirit alive in the Gilliland family.

Contents

Introduction **1**
1 A Coon in My Coveralls **3**
2 A Tribute to Man's Best Friend **6**
3 Amateur Fish Relocation Program **10**
4 Bee Bustin' **14**
5 Charlie and the Salesman **17**
6 Coon Hunting Mules and Labradoodles **20**
7 Don't Wake a Sleeping Skunk **24**
8 Doomed from the Start **27**
9 Farm Kid Rabbit Huntin' **31**
10 Farm Pond Olympics **35**
11 Farming Everglades Style **38**
12 Feral Fowl **41**
13 Firewood Follies **45**
14 Golf through the Eyes of a Hunter **50**
15 Hillbilly Birding **53**
16 Hillbilly Hunter Hacks **57**
17 It's a Bird…It's a Plane…It's a PETA Drone! **60**
18 It's Sooo Dry That… **64**
19 Katfish the (Canine) Gator **67**
20 Larry and the Muskrat **71**
21 Mutts I Have Known **74**
22 Ol' Stumpy **75**
23 One Hundred and One Uses for a Feral Cat **82**
24 Pest Hunts **85**
25 Rattlesnake Relocation Project **89**
26 Sometimes Life Just Stinks **93**
27 The Great Coon Bait Caper **96**
28 The Midnight Perils of Hunting Frogs **99**
29 The Thrill of Road Kill **102**
30 The Road Kill Game **106**
31 'Twas the Night before Christmas **109**
32 Wacky Warnings **112**

33 What a Teal Deal! **115**
34 Xtreme Wildlife Rescue **119**
35 You Don't Say! **123**
36 You Just Might Be an Old Fisherman if... **125**

Introduction

The skunk looked me straight in the eye as I crept slowly toward the cage trap. I hoped to quietly open the cage door, as I had done successfully several times in the past, and offer the little blighter his freedom. That morning as time stood still and a pale yellow mist suddenly filled the air, I learned a skunk can still spray you even as it looks you square in the eye!

While growing up in central Ohio, I discovered that every time I ventured outdoors to hunt, trap or fish, something hilarious would happen or my best intentions would go wrong. Imagine my surprise and joy to find that these same dysfunctional and amusing predicaments happen to all outdoorsmen! I was in good company.

I began writing about my outdoor experiences, both good and bad, to encourage readers not to let an outdoor adventure gone wrong keep them on the couch.

Fifteen years ago I submitted a story about an ice-fishing trip to a new publication here in central Kansas, *The Rural Messenger*. Mike Alfers, the owner and publisher liked it, agreed to use it, and launched my weekly outdoor column "Exploring Kansas Outdoors." Today, nearly a dozen papers in central, south-central, and western Kansas carry this weekly column.

About ten years ago, while hunting rattlesnakes in western Kansas, I came upon a copy of *The Territorial Magazine,* published quarterly in Dodge City, Kansas. A phone call got me a gig writing for that magazine, an outdoor humor column called "Outrageously Outdoors." From that column, the stories in this book describe zany "take-offs" and "what-ifs" about many of my mishaps and escapades in God's outdoors, from my youth until today.

If you recognize your own adventures gone wrong in these outdoor stories or find that your mind conjures up some of the same ludicrous scenarios as mine does, you'll discover that you're in good company, too. Even if you don't, you'll still get a chuckle over my mishaps. So make a root beer float, grab a handful of jerky sticks, and sit back and enjoy *A Coon in My Coveralls*.

1
A Coon in My Coveralls

One of Groucho Marx's more famous lines was "I once killed an elephant in my pajamas; what he was doing in my pajamas I'll never know!"

Each year when I sell the fur I've trapped, I recall an encounter I had with a pet raccoon when I was young. For the purpose of this story, I'll call him "Lucky" because he could just as easily have been the cuffs and collar on someone's jacket.

My brother and I trapped a lot and we soon found that fur became more valuable after trapping season was over because the prices were higher then. We skinned the furbearers we caught and learned how to properly stretch and care for the pelts, so they could be kept and sold when the fur prices were the best.

There were a few local places that bought and sold fur, some more reputable than others. One guy had set up shop in an old, round grain bin and actually showed me the shotgun he rigged each night to shoot any "unsuspecting" thief who might open the door, but that's another story in itself. One of the better-known fur buyers in our area was Mr. Squires, near the little town of Chesterville.

One particular winter day I arrived at Squires' place bearing my hard-earned collection of pelts to sell. The day must have been chilly, because I wore the standard winter attire of all farm kids—insulated coveralls. I've always been warm-blooded, and I often wore my coveralls zipped open in front. Today as I watched him grade the fur, I stood with my hands in my unzipped-coverall pockets and leaned against the front of a long, tall work table, which caught me about waist high. Suddenly, from somewhere behind the counter—but seemingly out of

nowhere— emerged an immense living ball of fur and dove headfirst into my open coveralls! I stared down in disbelief at the furry tail and wiggling derriere and somehow identified them as belonging to a raccoon. Now, raccoons are not all that large, but picture one coming at you from waist high and diving headfirst into your drawers! Believe you me, this one was immense!

Anyway, somehow I composed myself enough to pluck the wriggling beast from my bloomers, and after I had "freshened up" in the men's room, and ol' Squires had stopped rolling on the floor, I got the story on the coon.

As I recall, Squires said that some kids had stopped to see him one evening after checking their traps and told him they had a raccoon to sell. He told them to bring it in, and they replied that it was "still kinda warm." Squires said he was not concerned because most kids just had a few traps to earn a little extra cash, so it was common for him to get carcasses that had been freshly killed and removed from a trap. However, the "carcass" they brought in was very warm—and very alive! They had stumbled onto a young raccoon—I believe while cutting fire wood—and didn't want to kill it, so they decided they would just sell it to Squires and let him decide its fate. Its fate, whether good or bad, was to become a pet (or pest as the case may be) and to terrorize all who came into Squires' shop to sell fur!

Though embarrassing to me (in more ways than one) and hilarious to him, Squires said that my reaction to Lucky's sudden appearance over the counter was one of the milder he'd seen. If you can get past the fact that raccoons are into everything, and that there are very few doors or lids made that they cannot learn to open, they make good pets, and Lucky seemed to be no exception. Squires said the rougher you played with ol' Lucky, the better he liked it.

Raccoons take sort of abbreviated hibernations, more like long siestas, off and on each winter. Evidently, Mother Nature still urges even pets to do this, and when he suddenly disappeared, Squires figured he had somehow gotten out the door or had crawled off and died, so he kind of gave up on ever seeing the varmint again, even admitting that he missed the little beggar. Squires also had a metal roofing business, and one day, while in the end of his shop where all the big rolls of roofing were stored, he happened to glance down into one of the tall rolls and, lo and behold, there was ol' Lucky, sound asleep, taking his wild raccoon nap!

Now, fifty years later, ol' Lucky has certainly left this world, and I'd say it's a good bet Squires has, too. I don't claim to know how the "animals in heaven" thing is going to work, but I do know that when I first walk through the pearly gates, I'll darn sure have my coveralls zipped up, just in case!

2
A Tribute to Man's Best Friend

As I sit down to tap away at this month's outdoor page, for some inexplicable reason I feel the need to pay homage to man's best friend, for nowhere is man's best friend appreciated more than in the world of outdoor sportsmen. They sit beside us in hunting blinds, often so close they're nearly beneath us. They help us carry our gear to and from campsites, the boat, the woods and even back to the truck when the excursion is over. They are perfectly at home in the pickup, whether in the back, on the floor or in the seat beside us. They require very little in the way of maintenance, perhaps an occasional scrubbing to keep them squeaky clean. Yet, these stalwart companions provide us with years of dedicated, selfless service. Of course I'm talking about man's best friend, the plastic five-gallon bucket.

I wish they had existed when I was a kid. Oh, we had five-gallon buckets, but not plastic. Dad had a hanging feed bunk in the barn and if you couldn't surprise the steers and beat them to the bunk at feeding time, the only way to survive the ordeal was to beat them out of the way with the bucket. I ruined more metal buckets than I care to remember by beating cows with them. Had they been plastic, they'd have lasted forever. But, like I stated above, no one depends upon plastic five-gallon buckets more than the outdoor sports enthusiast. They come in white, gray, green, black, and camouflage. They can have metal handles or plastic. They are the ultimate rear rest / foot rest / equipment carrier rolled into one.

No fisherman worth his or her fish and chips will have less than half a dozen, and that's just in the boat. Be sure to designate one on the boat for those inopportune times when the need arises to relieve yourself of your morning coffee while fishing. If you're lucky you might get your wife or girlfriend to use one also instead of having to run to the dock when they get nature's call.

Although a tad large, five-gallon buckets also work well for bailing out water rushing into the boat when you fail to put the drain plug back into the drain hole in the transom before leaving the dock. When ice fishing, two nice white buckets (to color coordinate with your surroundings) will carry your rods, tackle, bait and lunch onto the ice. One turned upside down will then become your seat, while the other holds your fish. Fitted with a lid of some description, one bucket can do both. When a fish is caught, simply jump up, lift the lid, deposit the fish then close the lid and repose yourself again. For you intense ice fishermen (you know who you are) this also hides your catch from prying eyes. In any fishing situation, plastic five-gallon buckets are the ideal tool for transporting fish. Once home, they again spring into action as the supreme vessel to hold all the "by-product" of cleaning your catch. Bass Pro even sells a fish-cleaning board specially made to fit the top of one. I also found a kit containing all the necessary parts to turn a five-gallon bucket into an aerated bait container.

Though fishing seems to bring out the best in five-gallon buckets, hunters also benefit from them. Again, they are the cat's meow for

carrying equipment to and from a blind or stand. To carry all my trapping supplies I use one fitted with a canvas tool carrier. Though small camp chairs are probably more comfortable for a long wait, the buckets again excel as seats. Cabela's offers a variety of seats, all made to fit five-gallon buckets. One named the "Silent Spin Bucket Seat," is equipped with bearings like a lazy Susan, allowing a hunter to swivel and see in different directions. This seat can be purchased alone, with an added storage pouch that drapes around the bucket, or with an attached "stadium" seat, complete with back. Kits are also available with all the components needed to convert our friend the bucket into a hanging deer feeder (a nice camouflage-colored number is probably best suited here.)

Not a hunter or fisherman, and feeling left out? Wait, there's more! What's the most logical use for a plastic five-gallon bucket around the campsite? Right you are! I found several products to turn five-gallon buckets into portable camp toilets. One called "Luggable Loo" is a toilet seat and lid that the company says, "effortlessly snaps on and off" any five-gallon bucket, and allows you to "Stop dreading the call of nature when enjoying your next hunting, fishing or camping trip." Now, if you truly do dread "the call of nature" you may have some deeper problems than where to answer it. Anyway, they should probably make one in pink for the ladies and call it "Luggable Lucy" (this might be just the ticket to get her to use one in the boat.)

Just remember, these things won't flush and don't set over a hole in the ground so you become responsible for disposing of the contents! Please take the high ground here and empty them at the camp's designated dumping station. Don't toss it under the neighbor's camper and try to blame it on their big dog.

On the Web, I also discovered a drinking-water filtration system, once featured in Popular Mechanics, called "The Mission Water Filter System," sold by the Eagle Springs Co. It uses chlorine tablets or household bleach and special filters, housed in—you guessed it—two plastic five-gallon buckets!

Now, even in the outdoor sporting world I imagine I've just scratched the surface as to the myriad of uses for the plastic five-gallon bucket; quite amazing, actually, from something that is usually a by-product itself. Think about it; we buy them full of some product, use the product, and are left with the bucket, which, in some cases is probably more useful than the product inside. So after you've read this, find your best friend and give them a little extra attention; kiss your wife and scratch the dog, too, while you're at it.

I guess I'll stop here to stretch my legs. My chair is broken, so I'm finishing this story sitting on a plastic five-gallon bucket. Now where is that Silent Spin seat I just bought?

3
Amateur Fish Relocation Program

Someone once said, "If it seems too good to be true, it probably is!" Keep that in mind as you read this story.

A good friend from church, I'll call him Bill, phoned me one evening last summer to tell me the township was replacing a bridge on the gravel road near his place. He'd been there to look things over and noticed lots of small fish, catfish he thought, milling about in the mud hole now created where the old bridge once stood. Knowing that the mud hole would be pumped dry to start the new bridge, Bill surmised that all those fish would be chopped up and blown downstream, or they'd be left to bake in the Kansas sun, so he was exploring the possibility of transplanting them into a relative's pond. Free catfish; it doesn't get any better than that!

I procured a seine net and furnished two pairs of chest waders; Bill put several plastic feed tubs full of water on the back of his pickup and we met at the bridge site. Now, I remembered the creek as it had been and naively expected it to look the same. What I found was a dug-out gorge with six-foot banks, twenty feet wide, forty yards long and who-knows-how deep, filled with water the color of chicken gravy. After assessing the scene and calculating the poor odds of our staying dry and netting any fish, we donned waders and blundered forth anyway.

I was the first to part the waters; I began sliding feet first toward certain doom and ended up bottoming-out standing navel deep in the gravy, but still dry and upright. Evidently Bill and I both have gyro problems as our balance stinks, and evidently Bill's is worse than mine because he took the same two steps and ended up horizontal.

You've heard of a ten-gallon hat? It was right about then that we nicknamed his waders "five-gallon waders" for obvious reasons. Now, waders have no drain plug or bilge pump, so once water gets into them it's there to stay until you remove and dump them. And water weighs about eight pounds to the gallon, so suddenly you're walking around with the equivalent of a small child hanging around each leg.

This excavated pool was dammed at both ends, so we unrolled the seine and began stumbling toward the nearest end. To scoop up any fish that were fleeing in front of us, we needed to get very close to land before we lifted the net. Somehow we missed the memo stating that the last few feet in this end of the pool had been scooped out to build the little dam to hold the water back, thus the water level suddenly flirted with the tops of our chest waders. With zero fish caught, we saved face and slowly got ourselves turned around to head in the opposite direction. The aforementioned memo probably also warned that chunks of the former old bridge still lay beneath the surface.

You know the high-school football practice drill where players must run full speed through two staggered rows of old tires lying on the ground? Picture us trying to navigate those tires buried in three feet of coffee-colored water and surrounded on all sides by a foot of oozy mud, and Bill with the weight of that small child in each leg of his waders. Bill's side seemed to be the worst, causing him to bob around like an empty bottle in a gale. It must have all looked like a scene straight from the movie "The Beverly Hillbillies Go Fishing." We finally reached the other end and were rewarded with two small fish, one catfish and a bluegill, for our trouble. The fish Bill saw from the bank were still in there somewhere, but with all the unseen underwater obstacles to navigate and our inept bumbling around, I'm sure they fled beneath and around our net each time in droves. What with all the splashing, laughing and floundering around, I'm a little surprised they weren't throwing themselves onto the shore in their panic to flee the approaching tsunami.

After a couple more bumbling tries, we had our system down and began to net fish with each foray. Finally the feed tubs in the pickup held several dozen little catfish, so we decided to make one final sweep and call it good. About then my side of the net caught on a rock, and no matter how much I yanked, twisted and pried, the rock wouldn't turn loose of

the net. I reached reluctantly down into the muck and felt the rock. It was oddly shaped and had jagged edges. Suddenly the net came free as if the rock had moved and, as I lifted the net to the surface, the rock came along and looked back at me. Yes, that snapping turtle was as big around as a steering wheel! After a short thrashing rodeo I managed to grab the beast's tail and fling it onto the bank out of our way. One at a time we clawed and scratched our way up the slick mud wall and rolled out onto the grassy pasture bank where our wives awaited at the pickup. They had tagged along for the entertainment and neither seemed disappointed.

The new home-to-be for our catch was a nice big pond just a half-mile away that was dug to provide fill dirt for the exit into town from the new highway. It was easy to get to and we parked on the bank just above the water; surely this would be the easy part of the rescue operation. The pond was new so the banks were still bare dirt and were a bit muddy. Bill and I hoisted the first tub of fish onto the ground and dumped the excess water. The ladies grabbed the tub and headed down the bank toward the water.

We had turned to fetch the next tub from the truck when gasps and groans from the girls turned us around. There they sat, literally on their butts at the water's edge, pulling and tugging on their feet as if to get away from some unseen force slowly sucking them into the pond. Bill and I exchanged curious glances and clamored down the bank. Their feet were buried in some sort of gray, putty-like mire that was as close to quicksand as I ever want to see. We tried everything short of hooking them to the pickup and dragging them up the bank. We each got our wife under her arms and pulled with all our might; we teamed up and both pulled on one wife at a time, but nothing worked; their feet were stuck-like-chuck. With all the laughing and carrying-on, I honestly don't know what kept Bill and me from getting sucked in, too. Finally they had to just pull their feet from their shoes, which we later managed to somehow pry from the quick-whatever-it-was that held them fast.

Now, remember the "If it seems too good to be true, it probably is" quote at the beginning? I haven't yet asked Bill for permission to fish there, and I'm scared to even go back. But I have this reoccurring nightmare about someone sneaking in there to fish without permission and being found a couple weeks later still stuck there in the quick-whatever-it-is. That stuff is better than any "Keep Out" sign!

The Bible stories tell of Jesus turning a few small fishes into enough to feed several thousand people, with literally baskets full of crumbs left over. Bill had several extra tubs of water on the back of his pickup—plenty of storage for just such an event—but I'm bettin' when he pulled up to his pond he still found only two small fishes and four fat tadpoles!

4
Bee Bustin'

Over generations, farm boys, country kids and outdoorsmen have developed numerous ways of entertaining themselves, many of which actually serve a purpose at the same time. One such activity, little known to the outside world, is bee bustin.' Now, the honey bee's contribution to life-as-we-know-it is not lost on me, and they are welcome at my plantation anytime. But the contributions of wasps and those big ol' wood bees the size of cream puffs that gnaw away at the siding on our homes is totally lost on me, so they are the quarry in the good-ol' boys' game of bee bustin'.

The object of the game is fairly straightforward and simple; swat those suckers into oblivion using anything available, without breaking windows or threatening life and limb of those around you, the first being the most important. The two most popular weapons used in the sport of bee bustin' are the common baseball cap (or just plain "cap" as my dad would say,) and a tennis or badminton racket.

First let's consider the qualities of the baseball cap. Caps are cheap and easy to find, plus all farmers and most other households already have dozens of them on hand. In the sport of bee bustin' a cap is held by the bill, so another plus is that one size fits all. Those hats made of thick, heavy material pack the hardest wallop, but those nice light ones with the mesh in them are fastest in the air.

When your quarry comes into sight (or sound) simply grab the bill of the baseball cap, wrest it from your head and swing it madly in the general direction of the enemy. One word of caution here: be sure to hit the target with the top of the hat, as hitting it with the underside may simply scoop it from the air rather than killing it. This could cause

the target insect to remain alive inside the hat when placed back on your head, making for an even worse outcome than if you'd just let the creature fly past in the first place.

Since the only hat I ever wear is a stocking cap in the winter (which by the way is really sorry bee bustin' artillery) my chosen armament for bee bustin' is the badminton racket, although a tennis racket, ping-pong paddle, dish towel, yesterday's newspaper or even the book you're reading right now will get the job done in a pinch. The strings on a badminton racket are closer together than those on a tennis racket, giving the user the best possible chance of connecting with an incoming bogey. When I was a kid we had nests of those big bumble bees in our garage every summer and that's when we found out how good a bee bustin' weapon a badminton racket was. A hit anywhere on the racket's surface would zing those big bumblers clear across the garage and bounce them off the far wall.

Form in bee bustin' is not important at all, as you're often caught off guard and have no time to properly get your feet under you and square-up your body for the shot. So whether forehand, backhand, overhand, underhand, firsthand, secondhand or dead-mans-hand, it really doesn't matter as long as you hit the critter the first time, if at all possible, as the more swings you take, the more ticked-off it gets. This is the rule no matter your choice of weapons.

There are two basic field strategies used in bee bustin': the "mauler-brawler" approach or the "chill-and-kill" maneuver. You can often hear the invader before you see it, and a mauler-brawler goes on the offensive with the first buzz. He grabs the nearest sanctioned weapon (which, if you remember, is anything you can lift) and wildly pursues the invader, violently lashing out in hopes the sudden assault will drive it away or a lucky shot will nail it. (A word of caution here concerning junior bee busters: they always choose the mauler-brawler approach, and given their short stature, wild swings with a badminton racket can put certain body parts of bystanders in peril.) A soldier employing the chill-and-kill technique freezes with the first buzz, slowly and quietly gripping their chosen instrument of death until they actually have a visual of the perpetrator, at which time they surprise the attacker with lightning-quick strikes.

So there you have an overview of the popular but behind the scenes sport of bee bustin.' I read lately where it is believed ISIS may be using carrier pigeons now to carry communications; what's to say they aren't using wasps and wood bees too? They could be outfitted or implanted with computer chips, or maybe that confounded loud buzzing they make is really code! I'll bet we could retrofit drones with fly swatters or badminton rackets and program them to kill wood bees and wasps....oh, but now that's just gettin' silly!

5

Charlie and the Salesman

One of my nieces raises hogs, and just this week my sister (her mom) brought to my attention that the hog show at our county fair is Sunday if we want to go. That reminded me of the following story from our youth. So make yourself a sausage sandwich and sit back and enjoy "Charlie and the Salesman."

We were about ten miles from the nearest large town, and our farm sat at the end of a gravel lane nearly one-tenth of a mile long. Though we weren't quite in the middle of nowhere, we could see it from our front porch. There was always livestock of some variety around because we five kids were all active in 4-H and FFA. One of the resident animals was a big, red, Duroc boar hog named Charlie. Even though Charlie, at over four hundred pounds, was just a big pussycat, that's still a lot of pussycat, so Charlie came and went pretty much as he pleased. This was before the days of one-piece fence panels, and woven wire fence was barely a challenge to him.

We soon learned that the rule of thumb was, if Charlie could get his nose through something, the rest of him would soon follow! We tried electric fence with equal results. If he got as much as a snout hair under the electric wire before he felt the jolt, it just incited him to continue forward, taking several feet of the electric fence with him. The bottom line here is that Charlie pretty much had the run of the place and ruled the roost.

As I remember, the reason we put up with him was because he didn't root or tear things up like you'd expect a four-hundred-pound hog to do. Since our place sat so far from the road, and Charlie being a hog and all, he evidently didn't have the ambition or drive to navigate his big carcass clear to the road and get into any trouble there either. He'd get out of his pen in the morning, graze around the barnyard and loll in the shade all day, then find his way back in again at night; quite unusual to say the least. All he seemed to require of us was his feed at night and a good belly scratch each time we passed him.

Mom had an upholstery shop built onto our house, and did a goodly amount of business, so there was a lot of traffic in and out of our long lane. Evidently, enough of her customers were from surrounding farming communities that if Charlie happened to be wandering about, they paid him no mind. Even the UPS drivers had learned to ignore Charlie when he greeted them from the middle of the drive. Occasionally, however, she'd get a visiting salesman from one of her fabric companies out of state, and those guys usually came straight from the "big city."

One particular day, while working away in her shop, she suddenly heard a vehicle horn blaring from the driveway. Looking out the window, she saw one of the big-city salesmen sitting in his van in front of her shop, one hand smashing the horn button as he peered frightfully out the driver's side window. "Odd," she thought. But even stranger was the

fact that the whole van was rocking and wobbling as if being shaken by an earthquake.

This is probably as good a place as any to stop the story and tell you a little bit about our mom. Mom was about as big around as a minute and weighted about as much. She was a small spitfire of a lady who always had a cup of coal-black coffee in her hand (probably explaining her feistiness.) She loved nothing more than creating elegant pieces of furniture for people in her upholstery shop, but all the while remained as common as a dandelion. She loved to laugh and joke and would rather listen to the rock-and-roll songs my buddies and I played than anything. In fact she once told me she wanted a certain song by the rock band Three Dog Night played at her funeral.

So there sat the big-city salesman with an expression on his face like his whole life was passing before him, his eyes as big as hubcaps, in his van that was rocking and reeling like one of those old coin-operated kiddy rides in front of the grocery store. Mom walked into the yard to unravel the mystery, and as she rounded the front of the van, there were all four hundred pounds of Charlie gleefully scratching himself on the front bumper! I'd love to have heard the conversation around the water cooler the next day that salesman was back at his company. "Come on guys, I'm serious! I really was trapped in my van in the middle of nowhere by Hogzilla! It was a huge, beastly red thing that weighed fifteen-hundred pounds and could look through the windshield right into my eyes! If you don't believe me go look at the red hair on the bumper."

Now, knowing my mother, that salesman sat there for a while longer— not on purpose mind you, but it would've been tough for her to chase away a four-hundred-pound hog and roll with laughter at the same time.

So goes the story of Charlie and the salesman. I don't remember what ever happened to Charlie, but he probably died of old age, as he may have even been too tough for sausage. And no, probably much to mom's chagrin, we did not play Three Dog Night at her funeral.

6
Coon Hunting Mules and Labradoodles

I have a confession to make: I hate horses! In fact I hate anything even equine-related! I guess it all stems from that fateful day when I was just a formidable child, and grandpa's pony scraped me off its back against a huge wild-cherry tree that grew in our barnyard. I was scarred for life; no really, the scar runs completely down my right side. Anyway, this is a big step for me to even admit my dislike of the beasts, because living here in Kansas and hating horses is akin to living in a retirement home and hating the Wheel of Fortune.

I grew up in central Ohio where coon hunting was a popular and noble sport, and an offshoot sport that grew out of coon hunting and was popular for a time was hunting raccoons from the backs of mules.

Possibly the funniest thing I've ever seen was a rodeo act that consisted of a tiny monkey dressed in a tiny cowboy outfit strapped to the back of a sheep dog. Sheep dogs are high strung and wired like eight-day clocks, and that dog worked like a good cutting horse. (Did I just use "good" and "horse" in the same sentence?) That dog changed directions on a dime, and each time it did the monkey was flung from side to side like a tiny rag doll. You tell me how the rider of a smelly, cantankerous, sweaty old mule in pursuit of a raccoon through briars, brambles, fallen tree limbs, swamps and hidden barbed wire in the middle of the night, no less, would be any different from that monkey strapped to the back of a sheep dog.

Here's my take on it all… Having fallen into the river or swamp at least once, skinned and dressed a couple big greasy coons, and all this after thoroughly enjoying a huge pot of Texas-style chili your buddy fixed before the hunt, most coon hunters exude some rather unique and horrible smells at the end of a good night's coon hunting. Why would I want to start my evening as a passenger on the back of a critter that already smells that bad from the get-go?

To me an ATV is the perfect hunting machine, but even my ATV has some customized add-ons in the form of those nifty plastic totes with the snap down lids that can be had for a song at Wal-Mart. Sooo, even if I were persuaded to swallow my pride, chuck my hard-earned self-respect and throw common sense to the wind long enough to ride a mule into coon-hunting combat, there would have to be some add-ons applied. To facilitate my easy exit in the event of an emergency, say my ride attempts to scrape me off against a wild cherry tree, I don't want my hunting gear hanging all over me. Rather, I want it stowed in something like a couple old milk crates strapped across the mules hips with bungee cords.

Then there's the issue of light. All coon hunters wear large battery powered headlamps. A small battery pack is fastened around your waist, and a light capable of casting a powerful beam is fastened to your cap or mounted onto a hard hat. How on earth would that ever work if the hunter were riding on the back of a mule? I can't imagine a mule would be known for its smooth ride, so it seems to me Mr. "bobblehead" coon hunter would be shining his headlamp about everywhere but where it was needed.

To solve this problem I say we mount the lights on the mule. Ace hardware has clamp-on trailer lights, you know, for when you get caught coming home in the dark after secretly dumping your deer carcass in the neighbor's ravine with your junk trailer that has no lights. Just jump out, clamp those babies on, connect the battery and go. Anyway, buy a half-dozen of those and get creative. Those big ears have to be good for something, so clamp one on each ear. Myself, I'd clamp the other four to the loose skin under each leg and shine them downward for ground-effect lighting, but that's just me. By the time I got through with my ride, it'd look like a transformer clomping through the woods.

Coonhounds are notorious for getting lost before the night's over. They either jump a wily coon that leads them into the next county, or they go silent so the hunters can't follow them. My buddy had a novel way of retrieving his lost hounds. He always wore the same old army jacket, and if his dogs hadn't returned to the pickup when he left, he

simply spread that jacket out on the ground somewhere nearby and in the morning the dogs would inevitably be curled up there on the jacket awaiting his return. Now, that's fine for coonhounds, but how would that work for "coonmules?" I'm not letting that sweaty old crank curl up on anything I own, much less a good jacket.

And I can only imagine what would happen if someone found the thing standing in the middle of the road. Spotting a coonhound in the middle of the road would not seem too strange. But topping a hill on a country road in the middle of nowhere at three A.M. only to spot my coonmule standing in the road in front of you lit up like a four-legged Christmas tree with high beams shooting out from both ears and all four armpits? You'd have to change shorts immediately, and I guarantee you'd be in the front pew the following Sunday.

So far I've railed pretty badly against the poor mules, but as I search my soul, I have to say their tainted reputation is probably not all their fault. I think the name alone gives them a bum rap. I mean really, what does the word "mule" conjure up for you? It's right up there with other one-syllable, four-letter words like carp, crap, lard, lump, toad & turd. Just because mules are a cross between a male donkey and a female horse, why curse them from birth with a name like "mule." After all, dogs are cross bred all the time and given fine exotic names that use parts of each breed, like Afador, Cockapoo, and my personal favorite, a cross between a Labrador retriever and a Poodle, the Labradoodle. Why not be a little more creative and help lift the beast's self esteem with a fine and noble name like Donkhorsey or Hordonk or... maybe not!

Anyway, I know Donkhorseys and Hordonks make great working steeds and excellent pulling teams, but as far as riding them into the woods in the middle of the night as a way of chasing coons and following coon hounds, not so much! The way I see it, riding a mule to follow a coonhound ranks right up there with using a Labradoodle to chase the coon. A nickname my grandmother had for our feet was "shanks horses," and as far as I'm concerned, shanks horses are the only thing I'll ride into the woods chasing a coon, thank you very much!

7

Don't Wake a Sleeping Skunk

I recently agreed to see if a skunk needed eviction from beneath a friend's empty home that is for sale. She said she was in the house the other day and it smelled terribly "skunky" inside, making her think one might be living under the porch. My glasses have transition lenses that turn terribly dark in the sunlight, so as I blindly peered into the darkness beneath the porch, I wondered aloud how bad the situation might become if I suddenly came face-to-face (and hopefully not face-to-butt) with the resident skunk.

I've had some interesting adventures involving skunks in traps, the worst of which led to a drive home in my underwear, so I didn't spend very long looking beneath my friend's porch. Looking back, I can call them interesting now, but at the time my descriptions were slightly different. Skunks are fairly laid-back critters and, if caught in an enclosed or covered cage trap, can usually be carted away in the trap and unceremoniously dumped somewhere without incident.

Some years ago as a new trapper, I caught one in a large cage trap set for bobcats, possibly a first for both me and the skunk. As I slowly approached the cage, the silly thing ran to the back and began an acrobatics display fit for a circus. First up one side, across the back by its front claws then down the other side it went, twirling like a little black and white ballerina. With great effort and a long stick I got the cage door propped open, then turned and ran cause' I knew Pepé would be charging the open door for his freedom. At a safe distance I turned to watch, and there it still hung like Spiderman on the inside of the cage.

My next plan involved rushing the cage, arms flailing and shouting at the top of my lungs, hoping to scare the critter out the open front door. It didn't take me long to see how this would turn disastrous and the maneuver was called off in mid-charge. I had other traps to check, so I opted to leave for awhile, then just stop on my way back through and reset the trap after Pepé had vamoosed. A half hour later I found it still in the trap, curled up in a fuzzy little black and white ball in the back corner of the cage. I finally just left and the thing vanished sometime overnight.

My latest encounter was just last season. A short distance from town I had a large skunk caught in a foothold coyote trap. Despite most people's thinking, foothold traps usually cause a critter no more than a sore foot for awhile, but this skunk appeared to be stone cold dead. I stood and marveled at its beautiful silky fur as it rippled in the wind and tried to figure what had caused its demise. It had the trap completely covered so I needed to push it aside to remove it and prepare it for the fence row.

Like I said before, both the skunk and the trap were going to stink already, and not anxious to drive home again in my stocking feet, I found a nice sturdy stick to roll it out of the way. I don't know who was more surprised, the sleeping skunk when I poked it with the stick or me when it suddenly jumped to its feet! This encounter did NOT end in disaster (for me) but it gave new meaning to the old cliché, "Things are not always as they seem."

I've never understood how the term "skunked" came to mean basically getting nothing, as in getting "skunked" on a fishing trip. They are

amazing little creatures that are very good at doing what God created them to do. Their fur is soft and silky, their essence is prized by trappers and they're actually fun to watch as they waddle along. But if you ever get "skunked" by messing with one, I guarantee you'll get way more than nothing!

8
Doomed from the Start

One cold, frosty December morning a few winters ago, I slowly steered my pickup into the midst of several weathered old hay bales, and stepped out into the crisp, pre-dawn air. With the full moon illuminating the landscape like a spotlight and the frost making everything underfoot crunch like cornflakes, slipping in to our deer blind unnoticed this morning would be like trying to slip into the house past mom when I was a kid and had stayed out past curfew. It was the last Saturday of deer rifle season and my heart was not really in it, but the little guy on my left shoulder kept hollering in my ear "No deer yet this year? What a loser!"

I gathered my gear and began the short trek that would take me through a stretch of soybean stubble, across a small, grassy meadow, down a creek bank and up the other side to the blind. To the right of our blind lay a small woodlot that was a popular bedding area for the local deer, so my goal was to slip in quietly and catch early morning browsers as they left the area to feed.

I crossed the stubble field and, as I entered the meadow, I began hearing a strange, quiet sort of popping sound—like one of those kids' push toys that pops a ping-pong ball around inside it as it's pushed across the floor. At first I thought it was my insulated coveralls rubbing tufts of frosted grass as I walked, but that couldn't be, because the moonlight was so bright I could sidestep everything noisy. Or maybe it was just my old arthritic joints cracking and popping like Jiffy Pop popcorn with every step, but I stood still for a while and the sound still continued. Baffled at what I heard, but figuring I was making who-knows-what kind of noise because of my Bull-in-a-China-Closet syndrome, I strode onward.

I'd taken just a couple more steps when an enormous eruption somewhere in front of me stopped me cold. I instinctively reeled backwards and, staring skyward, found the bright moonlit sky filled with the huge, black shapes of wild turkeys, looking for all the world like beach balls with wings as they scattered to the four winds. Then it hit me that I had heard hen turkeys make that familiar quiet popping sound as they milled around me during turkey hunts. For anyone who has never seen or heard wild turkeys come down from a roost in the morning, it's about the loudest, most awkward and unscripted event you'll ever witness, and that's when it's planned by the turkeys themselves and not because of some intruder like me.

When the dust settled, the moonlight revealed numerous more roosted in the trees all around me. I remember starring at all those black shapes in the trees and thinking "This ain't gonna end well," when, like shots from a roman candle, every few seconds another group would leave their perches and scatter in a different direction. And finally, as if any deer were still left in this township, the last group set sail and glided right through the middle of the very woodlot I'd hoped would produce a deer for me this morning!

Now, the little guy on my other shoulder patted me on the back and said "Just go back home to bed; you tried but your hunt is surely ruined for the morning." I've seen too many situations where logic would have deemed the little guy right, only to bag a deer or shoot a coyote shortly thereafter, so I regained my composure, readjusted my now warm, wet, shorts, brushed the little guy off my shoulder onto the ground and continued on.

Next came the creek; we had pruned limbs to clear a path and formed steps into the creek bank, all in the name of getting to the blind quietly in the dark, even though that was obviously not a consideration anymore this morning. I shone the flashlight down into the creek, and what had been a dry creek bed before a recent rain was now a frozen moat. Given my luck so far this morning, it was probably full of alligators lurking beneath the paper-thin ice, just waiting for an errant deer hunter to fall through into their lair. It was already going to be a little uncomfortable sitting in the blind in warm, wet drawers, so the last thing I needed now was to add two wet, muddy boots to my outfit or to lose a

leg to a rare Kansas ice-gator, so I opted to go around. That meant crossing the meadow again, crossing the creek at a nearby culvert and taking the long way around, all in the bright moonlight. The upside was that there were probably no more turkeys left to spook. The downside was that there were probably no more deer left to spook either! To any deer that might have stopped for a look back as they left the county, the bright moonlight probably made me look like I was wrapped from head-to-toe in blinking white Christmas lights.

Our blind was a trailer with a camper shell on top and two sliding windows in front. The insides of all the windows were frosted over, which we are used to, but as I tried to slide open the two front windows, I found them frozen shut (well of course they were.) I found an ice scraper, and placing it sideways against one of the windows, I proceeded to rap on it with my fist until, one-at-a-time, both windows broke free and slid open. Now, any living thing not spooked from the property by the turkey explosion or rousted from the area by the eerie, hulking figure wrapped in white Christmas lights was surely driven from the territory by the sound of a jack-hammer being run from inside our hunting blind.

At this point, I might as well have stood on top of the trailer and sung the Star Spangled Banner at the top of my lungs as the sun came up, or built a roaring fire in the middle of the stubble field and danced around it to the beat of a thousand native drums; it would have made little difference in the outcome of my Saturday morning deer hunt.

A couple hours later as I walked to the truck, my once-wet shorts now frozen and crunching with every step, the little guy on my shoulder continued to holler in my ear "No deer yet this year? What a loser!" Sometimes all the preparation in the world just can't outwit Mother Nature. I flicked the little guy off my shoulder again, hoping the turkeys would get him as they came back later to feed.

9

Farm Kid Rabbit Huntin'

It's a wonder anyone from my era still survives; we grew up knowing there was a right and a wrong, we knew we were supposed to respect authority (whether or not we did,) we rode in the back of pickups and we even drank from garden hoses. We were happy havin' a few rag-tag coon and muskrat traps and a shotgun.

In high school, two of my constant companions whom I'll call Ralph and Mike for this story ('cause those really were their names,) came from a huge gaggle of brothers and sisters who lived a couple roads over and actually did occasionally have to hunt for their supper. Now, Ralph had an old scratched-up, battered 12-gauge single shot that fell apart into two pieces to load instead of just hinging open like it was supposed to.

We used to go to "turkey shoots" each fall where contestants were each given one shotgun shell to shoot at a paper target. The winner was the shooter who put the most pellets in their target. I'll never forget the looks Ralph would get each time he'd sidle up to the shooting line beside a dozen other shooters, then plop the ol' 12-gauge into two pieces to put in his shell. Muffled snickers would echo up and down the shooting line as all the other fellas with their thousand-dollar skeet guns watched in disgust. The boys became silent however when he won every round. That was the straightest shootin' old canon ever made.

During the 1960s there was an oil boom where we lived in Morrow County, Ohio, and either there were no regulations on anything or no one followed them, because oil rigs appeared on tiny podunk patches of ground barely big enough to contain the equipment, and the drilling rigs were so thick and close together, that at night the countryside lit up like the Emerald City. A company drilled a well on our place and told Dad they hit oil, but one morning we awoke to find everything gone, oil tank and oil included, without Dad ever seeing a cent. The area was left a mess, with lengths of oil-well pipe, huge wooden timbers and chunks of steel cable lying everywhere in the weeds. Dad decided he was going to get something from them for our trouble and, thinking surely they would come back and clean up their mess, he hooked the tractor onto several, long oil-well pipes and drug them to the other end of the farm and deposited them along a fencerow out of sight.

One of our favorite winter pastimes was rabbit hunting. We didn't have a dog, so we'd just wander through the woods and along fencerows looking for tracks and rootin' through weed and briar patches to kick out rabbits hiding therein. One snowy Saturday afternoon Ralph and I departed on a rabbit-hunting excursion that followed our usual route, starting behind the barn and turning right at the end of a short pasture, then following a drainage ditch that was overgrown on both sides with all manner of briers, blackberries and other stellar, rabbit hiding places. Several inches of soft snow made for slow going, but the snow made rabbit tracks show up like chocolate chips in pancakes. The drainage ditch ran for a couple hundred yards and where it ended against the next fencerow was where the high jacked oil-well pipes resided. Rabbit tracks littered the ground all around the pipes; one pipe in particular had a highway of tracks going into one end but none going out the other. A quick glance inside showed complete darkness, telling us Br'er Rabbit was certainly holed up inside. Eureka! But it seemed terribly unsportsmanlike, even to us, just to shoot him in the pipe, not to mention a complete waste of tasty rabbit meat, so how would we get him out? Surely pounding on the outside of the pipe would get him moving.

With Ralph standing near one end, his old 12-gauge canon at the ready, I proceeded to jump around on the pipe. I tap-danced, kicked, beat and pounded all up-and-down one end of the pipe—but nothing. Since we couldn't actually see him in there, maybe he was facing the other direction, we thought, so we traded ends and tried again—still nothing. Somewhere we found a long stick of some sort that reached part way through the pipe. While Ralph stood on guard, I poked and prodded from both ends, but still nothing! Curses, we were gettin' nowhere! Then

suddenly I had a two-word epiphany that would solve our problem: John Deere!

We hiked back to the barn, started the old JD 3010 with a loader on front and headed through the snow back to the pipe. As we chugged along we could almost taste the freshly fried rabbit, as surely no cottontail alive could keep its footing inside an oil well pipe with one end hoisted toward the sky. I swung the tractor around in front of the offending pipe, slid the loader bucket beneath it and lifted it a few feet in the air, all the while awaiting the thunder of Ralph's old 12-gauge as Br'er came sliding out the other end. Nothing, so I hoisted the pipe even higher, and still nothing. What, had we found a bionic bunny with four-wheel drive? I dropped the pipe back into the snow, pulled it away from the fence and slid the bucket under the other end. This would surely do it, we figured. Once again I raised the pipe, once again awaiting the roar of the 12-gauge, and once again, nothing. I tried it all: jerking the pipe up and down, dropping it onto the ground with a thud, even sticking one loader tine into the end and whipping it up-and-down like a symphony conductor's baton, all with the same results—nothing! If ol' Br'er was in there, I suppose by then he was either dead or passed out from fright. It was about then the realization hit us that whatever was blocking the pipe might not be a rabbit, but a clod of dirt Dad scooped up when he drug the pipe to its new home, a nest of some sort or maybe a dead possum. Lucky for us it was not a skunk! (I have a friend who was bit by a skunk that came sliding out of an irrigation pipe.) Anyway, whatever was in there was either inanimate or dead and was not going to taste real good fried, so we accepted defeat and moved on.

Guys stake down old barrels in lakes as lairs for catfish, often noodling big flatheads out of them during the summer. Maybe we should have looked into renting out our oil well pipes to neighbors as "cottontail condos," accepting a bunny or two each year as payment. With all the forgotten, left-behind, oil-well pipes there must have been in that county, we could have had dozens, perhaps hundreds of cottontail condo rentals. We could have become real estate moguls while we were still in high school! Yup, I can see it all now: RM&S (Ralph, Mike and Steve) Cottontail Condos, the full taste of the wild for only half the work!

10

Farm Pond Olympics

When I was a kid I owned a big ol' jumbo, prehistoric, aluminum canoe that looked like it would have been more at home on four big tires and pushing a snowplow. Its saving grace was that it was also extra stable on the water. One particular evening my brother-in-law and I were anchored in the middle of Dad's farm pond, fishing. A boat anchor on one end and a big steel ball for an anchor on the other kept the thing from twirling around in the wind. We had multiple tackle boxes open on the seats, I guess to give the appearance that we were big-time contenders on the professional farm-pond bluegill circuit.

Anyway, as it was getting dark we pulled anchor to paddle the behemoth toward shore. My anchor came up with no problems, but the steel ball on his end was stuck in the black, oozy mud bottom of the pond. Wrapping the rope around his hands a couple times, he leaned backwards to dislodge the steel ball. He was built like a dump truck and, when the ball came free, he hit the other side of the canoe like a rodeo bull out of the chute, causing ol' jumbo to do the unthinkable and dump us both into the drink. There we were, bobbing around in the middle of an absolute flotilla of fishing lures—some floating and some sinking slowly toward the bottom, but all sporting at least three razor-sharp hooks. Now, Michael Phelps and all the star Olympic swimmers of the day could swim the length of Dad's pond as easily as the rest of us could walk across the kitchen, but how about swimming it through a scum of floating fishing lures?

Welcome to the first event in the 2020 Farm Pond Olympics, the freestyle lure swim. The swimmers can choose their stroke, but they have to stay on top of the water. We'll divide the pond into lanes with bailer twine tied to electric fence posts on each side of the pond. All shapes and sizes of floating fishing lures will be scattered over each lane beforehand, and at the crack of the starter's pistol, the swimmers simply swim to the other side of the pond as quickly as possible.

The event can be scored a variety of ways; most lures on their body, fewest lures on their body or certain lures could be given a point value and the winner would be the swimmer with the most points when the point value of the lures clinging to their body is tallied. The event could be made even more life-like by unceremoniously flinging each swimmer from a sinking canoe to start the race. Heaven help the swimmers with a hairy back; when they climb out of the pond on the other side they'll look like a lure display board at Cabela's.

The diving board at Dad's pond was an old steel frame with a big, old barn plank for a board. We welded the frame from stuff dug out of the usual farmer's scrap pile and carried it to the pond with the tractor and manure loader. It was on the dam, so the frame was made to be as tall as the dam. One end of the old barn plank lay across the steel frame and hung out over the water and the other end rested on top of the dam and was held there with a huge rock. It did little good to bounce on the board when diving because the old plank had zero spring to it.

I remember going to a nice swimming pool once with the church youth group and running out onto the diving board and pouncing on it like I did at the pond. The thing flung me so high I had a nosebleed when I hit the water! I once watched my buddy Ralph bounce off the end of the board as usual, then looked on as the plank followed him end-over-end into the pond 'cause the rock had somehow gotten moved.

Anyway, the next event in the Farm Pond Olympics would be farm-pond diving. The degree of difficulty will always be high no matter what dive they choose, and the chunkier divers will have a definite advantage in the event. We'll probably have to employ an extra person at the judges' table to keep an eye on the rock.

Dad's pond was chock full of pesky little bluegills and each tiny one we caught found its way into the nearby fencerow as a way to weed them out of the pond. We found out that smacking them with a canoe paddle was a pretty novel and effective way to get them to the fencerow, so the third event in the Farm Pond Olympics would be bluegill batting.

The event will be divided into two categories; land batting in which each contestant will bat his or her bluegill from the bank, and water batting where the batting will take place from a canoe. The batters can choose to have their bluegills pitched to them or they can choose the freestyle delivery where they throw it up in the air themselves before whacking it. Winners will be chosen for both longest distance and for highest flight, and naturally canoe paddles will be provided so that no one has an unfair advantage.

I've made my pitch to the International Olympic Committee, but I'm not yet sure if this Farm Pond Olympic thing will catch on. I figure we have ranch rodeos so why not Farm Pond Olympics. Anyway, if the 2020 Farm Pond Olympics become a reality, I'll be available to coach bluegill batting.

11

Farming Everglades Style

One of the many fond memories I have growing up as an Ohio farm kid was of something called John Deere Days. Back in my generation, local farm equipment dealerships were small and as numerous as ice cream flavors. John Deere Days was an annual winter event where all John Deere dealerships in Ohio (and maybe nationwide) circulated a film (now do you realize how long ago that was?) that depicted unusual and often unheard-of farming operations around the country and around the world. These were interspersed with clips that highlighted all the new John Deere farm machinery for the year, like combines with cabs and massive twelve-foot headers…YIKES! Of course the evening began with ham sandwiches and potato chips before the film.

The odd and extraordinary farming operations included stork farming in Europe (without storks, where would babies come from?), mouse farming in Minnesota (yes, there are people who actually raise mice on purpose), worm farming in Canada and my all time favorite, alligator farming in Florida. The farmer harvested eggs from nesting alligators, hatched them in an incubator then moved the growing reptiles into concrete pens. Eventually they were harvested for their meat and hide a few years later; akin to how ranchers in the Midwest run cow-calf operations, only with beasts that could take-off your hand or foot, leaving it impossible for you to ever get back on a horse. The interesting part was how the farmer interacted with his "breeding herd."

So picture this: the segment began with the farmer bouncing along in an old 1950-something pickup and then parking on the bank that overlooked a big swamp/pond. He got out and climbed into the bed of the pickup (amazingly he still had all four limbs) and began rattling around metal containers. By now we were all wondering what in tarnation he was doing, when out of nowhere the swamp water began boiling with six- and eight-foot-long alligators that crawled out of the water and swarmed around the truck like a bunch of herd cows. He tossed them fish like a rancher tossing range cubes of hay slices to a bunch of heifers; then they filled their mouths and slipped back into the water. He climbed back into the cab and drove off.

Here are the problems my twisted and pessimistic mind sees with this. Harvesting alligator eggs means "robbing" gator nests, plain and simple, and knowing my luck, I'd find the one momma alligator that was a "prepper" and living unseen underground with her eggs. You see the problem there? I'd dig into the nest and become lunch.

Next problem would involve the feeding process. As my luck goes, my "herd" would have that one momma that could eat fish faster than I could chuck them at her and she'd never have to get back into the pond; I'd be stuck in the back of the pickup. By then the others would be coming back for seconds, and I'd be out of fish. Remember these were pre-cell-phone days, so my only hope would be that my family actually missed me when I didn't show up for dinner (which would be debatable)

and they'd eventually find me curled up on the roof of the pickup, ghost-white and hypothermic.

Then there is the problem that I'm sure has been hotly debated through the ages: how do you work a herd of alligators? First of all, you'd have to be able to keep them out of the water. Maybe that's where the present-day term "drain the swamp" originated? Then how do you persuade a herd of gators to go where you want them? As passive as they might seem, I doubt they'd have any special connection with the farmer, other than seeing him as the "bearer of food," so attempting to lure them into the corral with a bucket of fish would probably not be the best idea. Do you develop a special breed of dog that's all bones with no meat and tastes really bad, removing the alligators' temptation to simply eat the wrangler? Yes, horses would probably be safe from snapping alligator jaws as they could outrun them, but the first time they spooked, they'd dump the rider right into the midst of the lumbering herd, never to be "herd" from again. Or maybe one of the beauties of alligator ranching is that you wouldn't ever have to work them or corral them at all…now, there's a novel thought!

Anyway, I guess that farmer had all those issues figured out, as do the alligator ranchers of today. But call me old fashioned; it's just that I'd rather raise something that I could reach through the fence and scratch now and then without fear of having my arm removed in return.

12

Feral Fowl

Feral is the politically correct term given to domestic animals that have become wild, sort of a tame-animals-gone-wild kind of thing. It's amazing to me how many feral animals we have from time to time here in the U.S.A. Some years back, the feral cat population in Wisconsin became a problem. Within the past couple few years, feral pythons set free by people who had possessed them for pets, were wreaking havoc in Florida by eating anything that moved. For years feral hogs have caused problems in many states, including parts of Kansas. Now, the latest threat to our society comes from Florida in the form of feral chickens. (Yes, you read that right, feral chickens.) In disbelief, I asked my friend "Mr. Google" about this and was shocked to find headlines like the following: (from the North Florida Herald) "Uproar over armed firefighters killing chickens by homes," (from the Key West Telegraph) "Wild chickens ruffle feathers in Key West" (and even from The Washington Post) "Georgia town torn over feelings for wild chickens."

Now, I can understand how feral pythons and feral hogs are a problem. After all, neither of these are something you can just plink with a pellet gun. However, I do have a bit of a problem understanding how a feral cat population can get out of control. Where I grew up, once a neighborhood cat was out of its own barnyard, it was fair game, and shooting wild cats along the road was a rite of passage. But when it comes to feral chickens, my country-boy mind is not allowing me to fathom how on God's green earth wild chickens were allowed to become a problem! I've always been proud of how we Midwestern country folk solve problems, so I have a couple solutions, both of which I might be persuaded to offer as franchises to all you entrepreneurs so inclined.

The first is somewhat of a culinary solution. You could build a fleet of those little carts like the hot dog venders use in New York City. Each would be complete with a Coleman camp stove encased in some sort of stainless steel contraption, you know to keep you out of trouble with the food inspectors and to make the rig look more up-scale, plus a big fiberglass sprayer tank for clean water (this will require cleaning all the herbicide from your tank first.) Your only other investments would be a large frying pan, a couple utensils, a supply of seasonings and condiments, a fifty-pound sack of cracked corn once a week and perhaps a bicycle with which to tow the rig around. Oh, and one of those old-fashioned chicken catchers you can fashion from a piece of heavy fencing wire will also serve you well.

Find a neighborhood with feral-chicken problems and get your rig set up early in the morning when the chickens first begin to scratch around. Scatter a little cracked corn around your cart, then simply stand and wait with the chicken catcher behind your back. As yard birds get within reach, lash out with the catcher and snatch them up by the leg. Spin around in place, clean and pluck them into a trash container hidden under the counter (after all, you don't want to offend the customers.) Now quickly rinse them, cut them up, bread the pieces and chunk them into your skillet full of lard already smoking over the Coleman and viola! Fried feral fowl! A cooler full of ice might also prove handy on busy days so you can catch several birds at once; otherwise simply catch them as needed. When you close for the day, simply dump the gut bucket into the nearest dumpster on your way home.

Don't be afraid to vary your offering either. For example, Kentucky Fried has Original and Extra Crispy; you can offer both Safe and Extra Risky. Long John Silver's has Chicken Planks: you could call yours Fowl Flanks or Chicky Shanks. Use your imagination when naming your business too, as the more exotic the name, the more attention you'll grab. Names like Freddy's Fried Feral Fowl or Bob's Broasted Bantys will certainly suck in the patrons.

My second solution is a bit more predatory in nature and not quite so subtle. There is no better chicken thief than a wiley coyote, and the last I checked, this country has plenty of them, too. So this year instead of turning all my coyotes into pelts, I'll keep them alive and develop a stable

full of already-trained, four-legged, chicken assassins. I know a guy at the edge of town who works out of a dark garage hidden in a plum thicket behind his house and seems to have an unlimited supply of electronic parts. He assures me he can take an off-the-shelf, solar-powered electric fencer, juice it up a little Tim Taylor style, combine it with a cheap GPS unit and a police Taser, plus rig it to work with a remote. I'll dart each coyote so they're sedated long enough to fit them with a small backpack containing the amped-up fencing unit. At the same time I'll install a muzzle-shaped apparatus with prongs sticking out from it that will keep the coyotes from munching on small children, but still allow it to easily ingest a chicken. Regrettably, that will also mean they can still inhale small pets like cats, but hey, we don't want a feral-cat problem either! It'd be sort of like BOGO nuisance control: Buy One (service,) Get One (free!)

Now, go to the same neighborhoods you would choose to set up your Fried Feral Fowl stand and release a few of your wired assassins. Early mornings will probably be the best time; the chickens will be up, but no one else will. The fewer people that see a coyote wearing a backpack stroll across their lawn, the better. Now go to the nearest greasy spoon for some scrambled eggs while your covert coyotes ingest a few feral fowl. After a couple hours it'll be time to head back into the 'hood and begin gathering your troops. The GPS unit on the dash of your pickup will show you where each trooper is. Merely drive as close as possible, hit the Taser button on your remote and the coyote will instantly become a quivering, shuddering, four-legged bowl of jelly long enough for you to swoop it up and toss it into the cage in the back of the truck. Repeat this until all the feral-fowl cleanup crew is gathered, then head home and go fishing the rest of the day while the coyotes relax in the shade and process the mornings take. These guys will also make dandy rabbit or rat cleanup crews as well. I recently saw a video clip on YouTube of a coyote running the streets of Chicago, where they have reportedly actually been released to help control a growing rodent problem.

Well there you have it, another case of good ol' American ingenuity and Midwest creativity coming together to solve a problem. Contact me now for your franchise starter kits and be prepared; you never know when a feral-fowl problem might hit us right here in the Midwest. In the mean time I'll be working on a recipe for chicken marinade, 'cause even though they might taste "just like chicken," I'll bet they're some tough old birds!

13

Firewood Follies

For more years than I wish to count, back when I wore a younger man's clothes and had a younger man's back, I heated my house with wood. You know the old saying that wood is the fuel that heats you twice: once when you cut it and again when you burn it. I believe over the years I've added some amendments to that fable. I lived back a terribly long lane that often filled with snow in the winter. I remember once when the man farming my land was clearing my driveway with his big snow blower after an Ohio blizzard. The machine sucked up a couple pieces of firewood that lay somewhere in the drive by the garage. I'm pretty sure he was hot about that, so that firewood heated someone who hadn't even cut it!

Back in those days I also had a younger man's common sense, and I'm convinced I have that and firewood cutting to blame for the fact that an x-ray of my 65-year-old spine looks like an old, dead cedar tree after a Kansas hail storm. Despite that, I still have fond, vivid memories of cutting firewood with Dad in his beat-up, old International Scout. I'm pretty sure that Scout came over on the Mayflower (if not the Ark), but he'd put our saws and extra gas in the old beater and I'd follow him with the tractor and wagon. More than once we had to unhook the wagon and pull the Scout out of snow he had no business trying to drive through in the first place.

One spot we cut firewood was a couple miles up the road, where we'd follow an old, tractor path up a winding hill into a hay field and cut in the woods surrounding the hay. I remember clearly once when we pulled into the hayfield to cut up several logs we had previously pulled into the clearing, only to find nothing left but tiny piles of sawdust where each log had been cut up and "rustled" by firewood thieves. We were both hot over that firewood and it was nowhere to be found!

I had a lime-green, Chevy "Love" pickup I'd purchased brand new. If you remember, it was a tiny little thing, perhaps the first of the small pickups, but it was a firewood-haulin' machine. It was small enough that I could "weasel" it into the woods around stumps and standing trees and get into places where no "real" pickup could go. I have pictures of it loaded with every stick of firewood it would possibly hold stacked neatly in the bed like a pyramid and piled higher than the cab; it looked like a pregnant lime as I'd drop the shifter into low, cram the accelerator to the floor and head for daylight.

I had ten acres of woods on my farm. One year during harvest I spotted a tree that had been uprooted and laid over on its side, still sporting a ball of roots and dirt the size of a Volkswagen and leaving a crater in the ground beneath it the same size. For some reason when I went to cut it up that fall, I walked there carrying my saw and gas rather than driving the lime-green wood-haulin' machine. I had gotten the tree all limbed and had started from the upper end to cut it into firewood pieces when something went wrong with the saw.

Not having driven the pickup, I had no tools, so this was going to involve a long walk back to the house. I started to set the saw down into the crater beneath the monstrous root ball, but for some reason thought better of it and instead dropped it behind a nearby tree. I walked to the house, retrieved what I needed, then returned. Then it happened: I stepped into the woods and my chainsaw AND the tree were BOTH gone! Somewhere I had obviously stepped into an alternate dimension; maybe I'd gone through a stargate or been sucked up by a wormhole. I didn't know, but they were both GONE! I turned around and walked out of the woods, thinking that because I am directionally challenged I'd entered the woods from a different angle or something. But when I walked back in, saw and tree were still nowhere to be found. I stumbled around in a panic. Could one instantly develop dementia? Could my already frail faculties have suddenly left me altogether?

Finally I said to myself, "Self, there has to be a logical explanation for this, so settle down and figure it out." I began to walk slowly in circles, looking intently all around me, when suddenly there was my saw, sitting

behind the same tree where I had left it (go figure.) But cross my heart and hope to spit, as surely as there will never be tofu in my house, the tree I was cutting up was not there! Had the firewood gods come down and taken it home? Had Mother Earth felt sorry for it and swallowed it completely? As I stood there wondering if I was on Candid Camera or maybe in an Alfred Hitchcock movie, something began to look familiar. Then I noticed my tree. Evidently cutting all the limbs from the tree and cutting some from the top had taken just enough weight off the main trunk that, while I was gone, it stood itself perfectly back up in the hole! Had my saw been in the crater, it would've been scrunched beyond repair, and I would have been hot over that firewood that hadn't even been burnt yet!

The biggest firewood-cutting catastrophe I've ever been a part of involved cutting a huge, dead wild-cherry tree across the driveway from our house back on the farm. My wood cutting skills were the stuff of legends once I had a tree on the ground, but I'm pretty sure I'm still today in the top ten list of "whom not to let cut your tree down." Like I said, the old tree was across the driveway from the house, so it should have been a simple matter just to drop it into the open field behind where it stood.

Like most old barns in that part of the country, our barn was designed primarily for storing hay, and still had the steel track high against the roof on which the old hayforks ran. These forks were used to unload loose hay from the wagons and to carry it up high enough to be dumped into the loft. A large diameter rope run through a set of pulleys and, hitched to a horse or tractor, pulled the loaded forks from the wagon up into the barn. That rope still hung high in the rafters. We had an idea!

I clambered as high into the tree as I could and secured a heavy log chain and then attached to it the old hay rope salvaged from the barn. Now remember, this rope was possibly used to lash Dad's old Scout to the deck of the Mayflower. One end was tied tightly to the chain, the other end to a clevis on the drawbar of the old Farmall "H." With Dad on the tractor ready to pull the dead behemoth away from the house, I began to cut. The diameter of the tree was more than double the length of my chain saw bar, so it was a slow process. I finished the notch, then moved around the tree and started cutting in from the backside.

As I reached the point of no return, I gave Dad the high sign, and he tightened the old rope. The dead beast of a tree began to list in his direction. Life was good! However, the smile on my face evaporated at the gnawing, snapping sounds of rope fibers stretching and breaking. I watched in horror as the old rope unraveled and ripped in half, leaving the outcome of this undertaking in the hands of my chain-saw prowess! Time slipped into slow motion as half-a-year's supply of firewood snapped upright again, then slowly headed for the house and power lines. We had never worried about the house, which was safe by a mile, but like a football protected by a fullback as he dove for the goal line, the power lines were tucked snugly beneath its branches as the tree crashed across the driveway.

Bad enough you say? Not quite, as the calamity had torn something loose somewhere, knocking the entire neighborhood out of power. Certainly bad enough now, you think! No, not yet. Because it was Saturday, the power company guys had to come out on their day off, not to mention the fact that the televised Ohio State football game was interrupted (you K State and KU fans can understand this I'm sure.) So to cap off my firewood-cutting career, I had succeeded in heating up our entire neighborhood plus the power company crew with firewood that hadn't even been cut yet!

There are other tales to tell about firewood-cutting follies, like busting out the back window of Dad's pickup with an errantly tossed stick of firewood, but I'll save them for another time. I don't cut firewood anymore, nor heat my house with it, but I do miss the warm, cozy heat given off by the fuel that heats you twice.

14

Golf through the Eyes of a Hunter

Recently I passed a golf course on a chilly Saturday and was amazed at the number of golfers braving the crisp winter weather to chase that little white ball around on what amounts to be nothing more than a huge lawn. It's always puzzled me how that game can be considered a good workout when the most exercise most golfers get is dragging their overweight carcasses in and out of the golf cart. Anyway, it all reminded me of my first and only brush with the game of golf.

Back in 2006, as a valiant attempt to add a little culture to my otherwise mundane and culture-less existence, and to further stretch the boundaries of my comfort zone—also known as free tickets—I attended the 2006 Senior Open Golf Tournament at Prairie Dunes Country Club just outside of Hutchinson, Kansas. Now understand, I don't know a fairway from a flambé, or a bogey from a booger. To me, a driver is the person at the wheel of a vehicle, and putter is something we men do in lieu of something constructive. Yet there I was, reduced to being part of a gaggle of onlookers sittin' in the hot sun called "the gallery." Even though I tried my best to fit in, I'm pretty sure I looked at that entire experience slightly different than most other people there. Allow me to explain.

Every golf course is littered with various sized pits of sand known as sand traps. When I looked at the sand traps all around us, all I could think was what swell little ponds they could be. Largemouth bass and those big hybrid bluegills would love nice sandy bottom pools like those. Wild turkeys take regular dust baths to help keep bugs out of their feathers; in doing so they carve out bowl shaped spots in the dirt called "wallows." I'll bet those nice sandy "traps" could draw every turkey for miles around, sort of like a communal bath. I'd also bet every female turtle in the county comes there to lay her eggs in that nice deep sand. Wouldn't it be a hoot to see a golfer swingin' away at turtle eggs, thinkin' they were his golf ball!

Much of the hilly terrain between holes was thick with sandhill plum bushes. I imagine the refined eye of any golf connoisseur saw this as garnish, part of the overall presentation. I saw it as a never-ending supply of plum jelly. And just think how many gallons of plums those guys could put in all the pockets in those golf bags they cart around with them everywhere. And what about sandhill plum wine? You talk about an additional revenue stream! Lots of those guys are drinking anyway, so why not open a small micro brewery there in the pro shop and they could be drinking home-grown plum wine brewed right there at the golf course.

The miles of neatly groomed footpaths amidst the roughs looked to me like great spots for coyote traps. I know from talking with golf-course employees that coyotes love to roam golf courses no matter where the course is. Heck, I'll bet most courses would even loan me one of their neat, little golf carts to buzz around and check traps, just to keep the occasional coyote from scaring the dickens out of patrons. The trees bordering the course screamed deer hunting to me, and I had a few good tree-stand locations picked out before we'd left. And I hadn't even thought about the turkey hunting yet!

Anyway, as out-of-place as I felt, I began to see that this game called golf has a lot of similarities to deer and turkey hunting. For example, we'd been advised to find choice seats and wait for the players to come to us. So there we sat awaiting our "quarry," on hunter-green-colored bleachers at the 17th hole, a spot where we could see action all around us. Not much different I'd say than puttin' up our camouflage hunting blind near a "hot" deer trail or a known turkey roost and marking time in anticipation of a good shot.

Speaking of shots, when one of us makes a nice shot and harvests a deer or turkey for the freezer, there are high-fives and handshakes all around. Those guys too! When one of them made an exceptional "shot" he'd dance a jig, shake everyone's hand and even tip his hat to the crowd. They even had guys who raised their hands to keep everyone quiet while they shoot. (Now, there's something my wife and I would both benefit from when we hunt together!) I must say, though, that their marksmanship

left a lot to be desired. Those guys all shot 64 or 65 times each day, and I didn't see one of them carrying any dead critters to show for it!

Yes, my playing golf at Prairie Dunes (Now, there's a mental picture) would probably be worthy of a movie. We could call it something like "The Clampetts Join the Country Club." I'd have to have a special custom-made golf bag with an extra pouch on each side—one to hold a deer rifle with a scope, and the other to hold a shotgun. I'm pretty sure I could get a fishing rod and traps in there somewhere amongst the clubs. I seriously doubt they would allow me into the clubhouse or pro shop, though, dressed in full camo and smellin' like coyote bait or deer pee. Although, now that I think about it, after playing 18 holes, some of the guys comin' off the course might not smell much better.

15

Hillbilly Birding

Every spring, weekend bird watchers all across America venture afield to enjoy their pastime. They don jaunty little outfits with name-brand sneakers, safari shirts and vests with lots of pockets and those floppy hats with a sun skirt that covers the back of their necks. Thousand-dollar binoculars, the latest in bird books, and cameras the price of my house with lenses the size of stovepipes complete their ensemble. In droves, they head off to nature trails and wildlife sanctuaries in hopes of spotting exotic specimens like Northern Orioles, Blue Grosbeaks, Eastern Bluebirds and Cedar Waxwings.

In an effort to continue our quest for a more cultural existence, Joyce and I, too, have taken up bird watching, albeit with slight differences. Our jaunty little outfits are worn-out, camo cargo pants, sweat-stained, oversized T-shirts from the nearest military surplus store, knee-high rubber boots from Cabalas' bargain cave, and big floppy safari hats we won at a National Wild Turkey Federation banquet.

Mounted on a garage-sale tripod is my 47-dollar, Fuji-Film camera from Walmart, and we really don't need binoculars because we usually watch buzzards, which are pretty easy to spot. Our bird book is made up of tattered dog-eared pages plucked from rescued paper-back, garage-sale books and stylishly bound together with staples. The wildlife sanctuaries we frequent more resemble ramshackle sheds and tumble-down old barns or highway road kill. Once in a while we'll extend our coverage area to include surveillance of handrails on the tops of local water towers, which often become evening buzzard roosts.

Our more cultured birding brethren pack all their high-dollar gear into a new minivan and head on down the road to neatly-groomed parks and wildlife sanctuaries all across the land. They park their rolling photographic studio under a conveniently located stand of neatly-trimmed shade trees. There they can either slide open the side door and set up shop within the comfortable confines of the van or deploy an attached, several-hundred-dollar shelter that allows them to erect their cameras and other gear completely concealed under the tarp.

We pack our stuff Clampett-style in the back of a rickety old pickup, complete with my wife Joyce perched back there like granny on a five-gallon bucket to keep things from flyin' out as we sputter down the road. Our favored destination is the nearest road kill that will eventually attract buzzards. It's easy to find flattened, poached, skunk and 'possum carcasses or dismembered deer remains along main roads, but buzzards dining on them are always chased off by every passing 18-wheeler, making it tough to get National Geographic quality shots. We've developed a network of livestock farmers and ranchers who allow us access to their bone yards, those livestock graveyards off the beaten path where we can roll in, quickly "throw up" (please excuse the pun) our 75-dollar, Tractor Supply hunting blind near a freshly deposited carcass and have the place to ourselves. Often those same ranches will also have an old dilapidated shed hidden somewhere on the property that has become a vulture nursery, providing us with hours of interruption-free buzzard watching.

There is a definite knack to setting up a photography blind near a livestock bone yard. For starters there's the smell; you can never go wrong by placing the blind up-wind of a livestock graveyard. On the plus side, I could go for days without showering and Joyce would never know. And those little indiscretions that happen in the TV room after dinner and get blamed on the dog are totally cancelled out. Then there is the matter of how close to get. Too far away and you risk missing all those warm, fuzzy, candid moments as the buzzards interact with one another. Too close and you risk having entrails slapped across your camera lens as fights erupt over who gets the smelliest morsels.

I read a story about a guy driving his new, expensive little convertible down a country road one sunny spring day with the top down. As he crested a hill, he surprised several vultures feeding on a dead deer carcass right along the edge of the road. They surprised him as much as he surprised them, and as the vultures scattered in every direction, a few

of them still had hold of "stuff" from deep in the bowels of the carcass. As they flew in all directions they strung innards across the road like a visceral volleyball net that the little sports car drove right through, as it all happened too fast for him to stop.

It's every birder's delight to find a nesting pair of birds and successfully document them as they care for and interact with their newly hatched chicks. The rarer the birds the better and, though it takes good fortune to spot them in the first place, the real reward comes after having the patience and the right equipment to photograph them over time.

For us, photographing one particular buzzard nest required more spelunking gear than photography equipment. Literally in the middle of a section of farm ground where a farmyard once stood is a pile of old lumber that was once a shed. It looks as though someone unplugged a big inflatable bounce house, letting it simply collapse onto the ground in a heap. In the far corner of the "bounce house" was a granary, one of those little rooms where loose grain was shoveled into it from a wagon. On the floor of that granary, amidst filth, dirt, who knows how many years' worth of buzzard poop and an old cowboy boot, sat a mother vulture on two eggs. Baby buzzards give new meaning to the phrase "humble beginnings."

Entering from the other end of the lumber heap still provided enough space for us to crawl back to the old granary where we got close enough to mom buzzard to pry her off the nest with an old board so we could see the eggs beneath her; she simply plopped back down on the nest and continued her vigil. Considering her surroundings, I'm pretty sure she was nearly varmint-proof, as no coyote, coon, or bobcat worth their carrion would ever admit to stooping so low as to drag a sitting buzzard off her nest. We were probably in more danger there than she was!

We kept checking back every few days and watched two buzzard eggs become two white, fuzzy buzzard chicks. Our goal was to follow them until they learned to fly, and hopefully photograph that process; after all, how do you teach a buzzard to fly? It's not like mom-and-pop buzzard can push them off a bridge or out of a tree. But alas, the last time we were there, the two stared down at us from the top of an old windmill that stood beside the lumber heap. They had gotten up there somehow, and I doubt they'd climbed.

Such is the life of a hillbilly birder; none of the frills, none of the glitz, none of the glam, none of the recognition—oh wait a minute, the mailman is at the door with a certified letter. Certainly it's a reply from Nat Geo begging me to let them publish some of the buzzard shots I just sent them; you know, the ones with the cow entrails swinging from the camera lens. I'll let you know!

16

Hillbilly Hunter Hacks

One of the buzzwords of late is "hack." Now, hack can mean something very bad, like your computer getting "hacked," meaning someone has digitally broken into your information, and now everyone in the township somehow knows the secret recipe for Aunt Agnes's famous potato salad and Uncle Oscar's deer jerky marinade, (even though they were both written on the inside of the kitchen cabinet door.) "Hack" can also mean a DIY shortcut of some sort, like how to use a roman candle to light the neighbor's wheat stubble on fire without even leaving your yard. But I digress, so now on to some hunter hacks I found, and some hunter hacks of my own.

More has probably been written about different ways to start a campfire than about any other outdoor subject. First off, no one in the crowd I hang with is gonna have need of a campfire except for rare camping trips with the family, then we'll start our fires with those neat gizmos called matches and lighters. We all have Little Buddy propane heaters in our deer blinds, and none of us have the ambition to climb Mount Everest or do anything where emergency campfires might be needed.

Nevertheless, I found hacks about using corn chips and crayons as fire starters. Sure they work fine, but what self-respecting hunter is going to waste good corn chips to start a fire? Eat the chips and light the empty bag; it works just as well. And as far as lighting crayons to start a campfire, once again it works great and they burn for a long time, but no hunter worth their jerky would dream of wasting a perfectly good crayon just to start a fire. They should be kept for things of greater importance like scribbling messages and phone numbers on the wall of your deer blind or for labeling packages of meat in the freezer so you can tell this year's venison back strap from the muskrat meat kept for next year's coyote bait. Another interesting campfire starting hack I found involves dryer lint; it seems dryer lint burns very well and starts very easily. It can be stuffed into empty toilet paper tubes or merely carried in a Ziploc bag and used right from there. Now we're talkin' something we all can relate to. I mean who doesn't save all their dryer lint and empty toilet paper tubes? Instead of emptying them into the recycle container and trash every couple years, make fire starters from them! But in all my trolling of the almighty internet, I did not find one reference to the most trustworthy tried-and-true method of starting a campfire ever—even used by our Native American forefathers. From anywhere in Kansas you would have to travel forever to hunt deer where there are no cattle nearby, SO LIGHT A DRY COW TURD.

The next most-talked-about topic in the outdoors, especially relating to survival, is how to build a shelter. Let me offer a hillbilly hack for building a shelter. All hillbilly outdoorsmen worth their pork rinds will

have a serious collection of tarps, and what a better use for a tarp than an emergency shelter. Harbor Freight has them in all sizes and you can occasionally get a small one "free with any purchase," so there's absolutely no excuse for not having one to carry with you on all outdoor excursions. A word of caution here: it's not in your best interest to remove the tarp covering the hole in your trailer-house roof. Anyway, there are a variety of ways to deploy your tarp/shelter. If you're fishing, I'm sure you'll have dynamite with you, so merely drop a stick into a small hole you dig in the ground, light her up and you'll soon have a nice cave that you can crawl into and cover with your tarp.

No friend of mine would be caught dead on a hunting or fishing trip without a menagerie of plastic five-gallon buckets, and the uses for them as hillbilly hunter hacks are endless. You can buy kits to turn one into a "luggable loo," and even cut a notch lengthways in a pool noodle and snap it around the top for a soft seat while you heed nature's call. Spray paint a few more green, drill a small hole at the bottom and put them at the base of each "illegal pharmaceutical" plant you "just happened to find growing" along the river as a way to water those beauties. Five-gallon buckets make great hillbilly mouse traps, too, for the deer blind or even the living room. On each side of the bucket near the top, drill a hole big enough for a broom handle to slide through and fit loosely enough to spin. Fill the bucket with water or used motor oil (which I'm sure you will have by the barrel-full,) put a glob of peanut butter in the middle of the broom handle and viola; when a mouse walks the broom handle to get the peanut butter, it will spin and dump the little blighter into the slurry below. If you keep the TV volume low enough, you can hear the splash and reward the cat with a live mouse.

I'm certain the list of hillbilly hacks, whether for hunting or not is endless, and I've probably just scratched the surface here. Maybe a book is in order, "Hillbilly Hunter Hacks for the Deer Blind, Boat, and Living Room." For all my loyal readers who want one, let me know and I'll reserve you a signed copy.

17

It's a Bird...It's a Plane... Nope, It's a PETA Drone

Some years back, the poor misguided group calling itself PETA (People for the Ethical Treatment of Animals, or as I call them: People Eating Tasty Animals) announced plans to purchase small drone aircraft to spy on hunters and factory-farm operations. The press release read "PETA will soon have some impressive new weapons at its disposal to combat those who gun down deer and doves. The group is shopping for one or more drone aircraft from which to monitor those who are out in the woods with death on their minds." I hope their liability insurance is paid up, because after reading that I was laughing so hard I fell from my chair and horsed up my back.

A few days ago, Jason Probst, fellow hunter and news editor for *The Hutchinson News,* wrote an editorial called "Open Season" in which he proposed creating a year-round hunting season for PETA drones, and thereby using this hilarious, thick-witted idea to help raise funds for our cash-strapped Kansas Wildlife, Parks and Tourism division. This all got me to thinking, and I can see an endless revenue stream, so here are some of my recommendations.

A special license will be required, allowing the hunter to "harvest" one drone. Just like deer and turkey seasons, additional "drone tags" can be purchased for a nominal fee. Legal hunting hours will be anytime you are awake, legal hunting equipment will be anything available short of a bazooka and there will be no possession limit (come to think of it, forget the bazooka-ban; if you own a bazooka you should be able to use it, too.)

Hunter's education will have to add a "drone identification" segment to its program. You'll need to know the difference between, say a PETA drone and the neighbor kids radio controlled airplane or your mother-in-law's satellite dish (on second thought, don't worry about your mother-in-law's satellite dish.) Proper marksmanship will also have to be addressed. You'll need to know just where to hit one of those little suckers to bring it down cleanly so you won't have to comb the whole pasture for parts and pieces before taking your prize to the taxidermist. This will actually create a few new jobs by hiring some of those tech-savvy, high-school nerds to act as marksmanship coaches and show us exactly where the sweet spot will be for a clean kill shot, and to work as "techsidermists," (that's a taxidermist for busted-up electronic stuff) putting our mangled drones back together to be mounted for our trophy rooms.

And of course a scoring system will be required to appropriately compare each successful drone hunter's prize against all others, much like the Boone and Crocket measuring system presently used to rate the size of big game animals. Since all drones are likely to be nearly the same, we'll have to get creative here. One category can be the number of parts still intact after retrieving each drone from the dirt: the more recognizable parts, the larger the score. A second category might consider the number of shots needed to remove a drone from its orbit: the fewer shots fired the higher the score. Along with that category, the size of the weapon used could also be considered. In my book, a drone harvested cleanly with a .22 rifle should outscore one cremated with a ten-gauge goose gun (which will probably also garner a lower score in the "recognizable parts" category.)

Drone hunting could also spawn a whole new industry centered on "drone guide services." Since I doubt this drone spying thing will ever really take hold, hunting them could be a rather specialized sport, requiring a few people to become quite familiar with feed yards and deer woods that are favorite targets of the flying little 007s (more jobs yet). Again, "techies" will probably excel at this, constantly monitoring the internet for PETA chatter and hacking PETA computers to determine when and where drones plan to hit, and relaying that info to a small fleet of guides afield with their hunter clients. Companies already make full-body deer targets and decoys; why not produce a line of deer and cow decoys adapted for a hunter to sit comfortably inside them as they patiently wait for the telltale hum of a trophy drone overhead. Then at just the right

moment, the head of the plastic white-tail buck or Hereford steer could be flung open, allowing the hunter to bring down the offending drone.

    Dogs can be trained to sniff out most anything from drugs to cadavers and to retrieve downed game anywhere, so why not also train dogs to find and retrieve downed drones? The dogs will probably be wearing little blaze-orange vests anyway, so let's fill each vest with electronic detection gear capable of sensing any semblance of life left in mutilated diodes and transistors, then simply teach the dog to listen to the equipment. Heck, PETA will possibly have homing devices in each drone to start with, as some will surely fall from the sky on their own. The techies will be able to figure out how to monitor that signal with their eyes closed, allowing one of the guides to retrieve it before PETA does.

    That alone could lead to an entire industry where assassinated PETA drones would be reprogrammed and used to spy on PETA itself. I can see it all now; as the top PETA clown works away in his office, one of his own drones suddenly appears outside his window carrying a box of steaks, a bag of deer jerky and an autographed picture of Ted Nugent.

And if one of those drones happens to fall into the hands of a bunch of good-ol'-boys, Katie bar the door! I have to assume they'll have recording capabilities, so once it's reprogrammed to strafe PETA headquarters and crash through the director's office window, the Power-Point slide show contained within will probably include, among other things, an inside shot of a freshly field-dressed deer, a coyote carcass being relieved of its pelt and I'm sure at some point a room full of good-ol'-boy posteriors.

My biggest fear now is that PETA won't follow through with this drone thing, and all this brainstorming will be for naught. I mean, look at all the extra cash that could be pumped into local economies for hotel rooms, guns & ammo, and license fees. And think of all the new jobs these things would create. Say! Maybe we taxpayers should invest in a few drones of our own and cruise them up and down the halls of congress. They'll never be shot down, and with cameras and recorders aboard, what REALLY goes on in congress will be all over Facebook and YouTube..... Thank You PETA!

18

It's Sooo Dry That...

I feel a little badly about writing this now that our area just had a nice rain, but there are still those who haven't, and maybe this will bring a chuckle or two to everyone. So knowing how dry Kansas can get, think in that context as you read.

Last Sunday after church, a western Kansas rancher and a visitor from Washington State struck up a conversation and the topic naturally turned to how dry it was there in western Kansas.

"Does it ever rain in this blooming state?" the visitor asked.

"Oh sure," answered the rancher. "Do you remember the story in the Bible where it rained for forty days and forty nights?"

"Yes, I'm familiar with Noah's flood," replied the visitor.

"Well," began the rancher, "That time we got about 2 ½ inches."

Someone asked me today if I'd been doing any frog hunting yet, being frog season is open now. I told them I would if I could find some water. I got to thinking that I should try the sewage-treatment ponds just outside town; there's always water there, and for that reason the frogs are probably so thick there we could catch 'em with dip nets. Besides that, they probably glow in the dark, makin' them easy to net, and I'll bet they have four legs t'a boot!

A new friend of mine, a recent transplant to Kansas, shared with me some pages from his diary:

June 10th – Just moved to Kansas. Now, this is a state that knows how to live—beautiful sunny days and warm, balmy evenings. It's beautiful! I love it here!

June 14th – Really heating up, got to 100 today. Not a problem, I live in an air-conditioned home and drive an air-conditioned car. What a pleasure to see the sun everyday like this.

June 20th – I had the backyard landscaped with western plants today, lots of rocks and cactus. No more mowing the lawn for me. Another scorcher today, but I love it here.

July 3 – The temperature hasn't been below 100 all week. How do people get used to this heat? At least it is kind of windy, though. Getting used to this heat is taking longer than I expected.

July 5 – I missed Lomita my cat sneaking into the car when I left for work this morning. When I got to the car after work, she had roasted to death, and now my hot car smells like grilled cat! Good ol' mister sun strikes again.

July 7 – The air conditioner shot craps and the repairman charged me $200 to drive by and tell me he needed to order parts. I've been sleeping outside on the patio for three nights now; a $225,000 house and can't even go inside! Lomita is the lucky one; why did I ever come here?

July 10 – Got the AC fixed; it cost $500 and drops the temperature down to 85. If one more wise guy asks "Hot enough for you today?" I'm going to strangle them. I hate this stupid state!

July 12 – My car smells like fried cat; my new air conditioner barely gets the inside of my house cooler than my morning coffee; my new cactus can't even live in this blasted heat; and the weather report might as well be a recording! Does it ever rain in this God-forsaken place?

July 14 – Welcome to HELL! Forgot to crack the car windows at work today and since it was 115, the windshield blew out. When the repairman came to fix it, guess what he asked me??? "Hot enough for you today?" It cost my sister $1500 to bail me out of jail. What kind of demented idiot would want to live in a place like this?

Just when you thought you'd heard every possible way to finish this sentence "It's soo dry that…", let me offer a few more:

It's so dry that the Baptists are sprinkling, the Methodists are using wet-wipes, the Presbyterians are giving rain checks and the Catholics are praying the wine will turn back to water.

It's so dry that cows are giving evaporated milk and hens are laying hard-boiled eggs.

It's so dry that the river runs only twice a week.

And finally, it's so dry that they've had to close two lanes at the local swimming pool and swimmers are actually encouraged to pee in the pool.

As a farm boy in Ohio, I thought the Ohio state fair was the perfect end to summer. We took our flock of registered sheep and stayed there for most of the fair. Just up the midway from the sheep barn was a dunk tank manned by a clown calling himself BoBo. Now, BoBo knew just exactly how to taunt kids to the point where they would spend their life savings just trying to dunk him. His famous one-liner that I can still remember echoing across the midway into the wee hours of the morning was "BoBo, High and Dry!" BoBo, I feel your pain!

19

Katfish the (Canine) Gator

Picture this: you're a law enforcement officer in Kansas City, Missouri, and you show up one morning at a home to evict the tenant, along with his belongings, only to find his "belongings" include a seven-foot alligator.

One Wednesday morning last fall law enforcement officers arrived at the home of Sean Casey in southeast Kansas City, Missouri, to evict him from the home he was renting, giving him just a short time to gather his possessions. They soon found his possessions included three python snakes, several domesticated dogs and cats, a rabbit named "Dinner" and a seven-foot alligator affectionately called "Katfish" found lounging in a hot tub at the home. (I'll bet anything the number of pets beside Katfish around the Casey household varied greatly from week-to-week depending on how hungry Katfish got.) The officers had to enlist the help of animal control officers and Dana Savorelli who operates Monkey Island, a local exotic wildlife rescue group. It took four men and Savorelli to remove the gator, and after a lengthy rodeo, Katfish was finally extracted from his cushy hot-tub hideaway and exiled to Monkey Island.

Casey got Katfish when he was only 15 to 18 inches long and now, four years later, he is seven feet long and weighs 200 pounds. Casey insists, "Gators are not big and ferocious like people think. Katfish doesn't seem to know he's an alligator and thinks he's a dog. He likes to come out and play and sit on my lap. Sometimes he gets kinda smelly, but he wags his tail when I come home." Casey said, "I tell people I have an alligator that can't swim and is afraid of the dark and of thunderstorms." Casey says he fed Katfish chicken nuggets, steak, deer, and fish.

Wait, what??? Yes, you read all that correctly. I don't understand how people don't foresee that a 15-inch alligator will eventually grow to be a seven footer. I mean have you ever heard of a "pygmy" alligator. You have to wonder if that part of Kansas City has a long list of unsolved missing person cases and maybe a lower than average homeless population, to boot. Good luck trying a seven-foot gator for homicide, but I'll bet high-profile attorneys from around the world would be linin' up to defend him. I can hear the opening arguments now: "Your honor, my client pleads not guilty. The state has failed to provide one single shred of evidence against Mr. Katfish. There were no bodies found, no murder weapons recovered and as for motive, well he was just hungry!" Then one day after a recess for lunch, the prosecuting attorney would not show up, and the rest of his legal team says he/she has just disappeared…wait, uh-oh!

I personally think Casey is being really naïve. I have to think ol' Katfish made secret nightly soirees out into the hood for snacks. I'll bet if you only knew, that neighborhood is devoid of most anything else on four legs but Katfish. Parts of Kansas City have a white-tail-deer problem and that would be a novel "natural" solution. Since Kansas deer have never seen the likes of a gator before, ol' Katfish could probably waltz right up to grazing white-tails, wish them a good evening and invite them for dinner…his dinner that is. It looks like the house where he lived with Casey is very near a pond and not far from the Little Blue River, so after dinner a short waddle to either body of water would allow him to dispose of any remains and no one would be the wiser. Katfish must have had a special "Don't Eat Us" contract with the rabbit named Dinner and with Casey, too, for that matter. After all, if Casey were to disappear, who would pay the electric bill to keep his hot tub warm? Casey told reporters he had made Katfish a ramp to get himself in and out of the hot tub and the house. So I guess theoretically after his late night banquet he could just drag his fat and sassy carcass back up the ramp, plop back into his comfy warm hot tub sanctuary, and life would be good; he'd be livin' the dream!

Evidently I've had this pet thing wrong for all these years. I've always thought pets should be soft, warm, and snuggly, not smell like the bayou, feel like the bark of a hedge-apple tree, and weigh a quarter ton. While I kinda like playing tug-o'-war with our little pups and having

them curl up on my lap in the evening, I can't wrap my head around playin' tug with a seven-foot alligator. The tug toy would have to be a good-sized tree. Can you imagine playing fetch with the thing? You'd toss the ball a little too far so that it accidently rolled off your property and out of sight, and after a few minutes ol' Katfish would come lumberin' across the yard, pleased as punch, with a couple neighbor kids in his mouth to drop at your feet. And as for wagging his tail when you came home, I'd be afraid to exit the car as that huge wagging tail would take me off my feet and fling me across the lawn or, worse yet, catch the side of my car and flip it over with me still inside. His treats at bedtime would have to be whole hams, twelve-pound turkeys, or deer hindquarters. And I don't even know what to say about the beast sittin' on my lap! I really don't want my headstone to read "Here lays old Steve, flatter than flat, they say his pet alligator crawled up on his lap."

As for his supposed diet of chicken nuggets, steak, deer, and fish—well, I can only suspect that Schwann's has a tough time getting drivers for a route through Casey's neighborhood. After the first time a driver comes back to his truck after making a house call to find Katfish pryin' the doors of the freezer compartment open and dragging out frozen dinners, meatballs and fish patties by the mouthful, that driver probably ends up in the local psych ward, never to enter that neighborhood again. I'll bet all fast food drive-throughs for miles around have Casey's picture on the wall inside the drive-up window with a caption reading "If this vehicle drives up, refuse them service as it may have a seven-foot alligator in the backseat that will take off your arm as you hand out their order of 30 dozen chicken nuggets."

Although keeping an alligator is illegal in Kansas, maybe I'm givin' ol' Casey a bad rap here. Just maybe he was letting Katfish grow as big as possible to become his retirement nest egg, so to speak. After all, have you priced Tony Lama boots lately or recently checked the price of alligator meat at a seafood shop?

20

Larry and the Muskrat

On hot summer days when someone asks me what outdoor adventure I found to write about this week, I just glare at them. Joyce and I are both cool-weather fans, and when it's much over 80, we become vegetables. So this heat drives me inside where I sit at my computer and ponder cooler days and stories from years gone by. One such story I often think about happened on a hot summer morning where I grew up and deserves telling again. It involves a high school classmate of mine, his older brother, and a muskrat. So sit back and enjoy Larry and the Muskrat.

John and I graduated together and were just a few years out of high school. He and older brother Larry both had bass boats and liked to spend Sunday mornings on a nice local reservoir named Clear Fork. Larry said he enjoyed the quiet time and all the wildlife he saw as much as the fishing.

This particular morning he was fishing with a spinner-bait, a large odd-shaped contraption full of hooks and shiny blades that makes the whole rig spin and chatter as it's retrieved through the water. He was close to shore and had stopped casting to watch a muskrat putter about along the bank. A few feet of line hung from his rod with the spinner bait dangling from the end. After several minutes of being amused by the muskrat, he decided it was time to fish again so he slapped the water with the spinner bait just to scare the muskrat. However, the line carried the lure farther than expected, mistakenly hooking the surprised muskrat, and the fight was on!

John was fishing a ways off, but the commotion caught his attention and the first thing he saw was Larry's rod bent doubly into the water. Between chuckles, Larry quickly explained the situation and asked for his help. John got his boat as close as possible and, after what must have been quite a tussle, he managed to dip the struggling muskrat from the water. But razor sharp teeth made quick work of the net and the struggling rat was in the water again, this time with Larry's line running through a dip net sporting a huge hole in its bottom. After another lengthy scuffle, they once again managed to somehow hoist the combative muskrat into the boat, and then the real rodeo began. Now, John and Larry were both avid outdoorsmen and conservationists, and all they wanted to do was unhook poor muskrat Sam without harming him. Like I said before, a spinner-bait is full of sharp treble hooks, and now they had one very ticked-off, soaking wet muskrat in the boat with several sets of those hooks fastened securely to him and he evidently was not obeying their verbal commands very well. Remember, Larry's line was still running through a ruined dip net that I'm sure was very much in the way.

Somehow Larry got the muskrat pulled back through the net and John was able to pounce on it, pinning the hapless critter to the floor with the rim of the net across its neck. John held it down with his foot while Larry went to work with his pliers attempting to extract the hooks. A fish with a couple hooks in its mouth is one thing, but a soaking wet

rodent the size of a loaf of bread with who-knows-how-many hooks fastened securely to its fur-covered body is quite another matter.

Larry worked feverishly, noticing that the muskrat's eyeballs were bulging slightly from the weight of John's foot on the steel ring across its neck. Each embedded hook had to be wobbled and wiggled until the sharp barb on its tip pulled free from the muskrat's tough hide. Finally success as the last of the hooks came free! But then there remained the problem of how to get one still ticked-off but now absolutely free muskrat out of the boat. With that quandary swirling in their minds, both guys simultaneously stepped backward to suddenly release the muskrat (in their minds somehow hoping it would just launch itself over the side) but looked at each other in disbelief as the poor luckless creature lay lifeless on the floor, evidently strangled in the process, despite their best intentions. Problem solved!

21

Mutts I Have Known

Not that many years ago I would have qualified as a "pet hater." I played no favorites; whether a guppy or a gerbil, a python or a Pekingese, a pot bellied pig or a Persian, I pretty much disliked them all equally. Events and relationships in my life had soured me on pets, which never seemed to like me anyway, so I figured "No skin off my back." Then six or eight years ago, my wife, once a card-carrying pet hater herself began liking the idea of having a dog around, and the rest is history. That dog and the two little mutts we have today, grabbed my heart and never let go. These are the stories of a couple ol' country mutts I knew before "my conversion."

Wimpy and the Woodchuck

Once upon a time, when men were men, boys were boys, and hay bales were still hay bales and not huge, immense rolls of grass, my summer income came from the same source as all other high school boys from my era: baling hay. We're talking wagon load after wagon load of over 100 square bales apiece, loaded on wagons pulled behind the baler, taken to the barn, unloaded onto an elevator, and stacked in the loft. Remember that? The farm boys in our neighborhood were the usual ornery, free-spirited lot, but we all knew how to work hard, (remember that too?) and come hayin' time each year, we became more valuable to local farmers than four-legged chickens.

Such was the case with Chester Campbell. "Chet" as he was known, lived across the road from me and, for reasons unknown, didn't seem to care much for us neighborhood boys. The feelings were mutual, but like I said, once his hay was down, we became angels with hay hooks.

Ohio has groundhogs like Kansas has coyotes; wherever there is ground there are groundhogs. Groundhogs, like Punxsutawney Phil, best known as woodchucks, look like overgrown prairie dogs, short stumpy tail and all, and can easily grow to weigh ten pounds or more—and rumor has it they do taste just like chicken. They have two sharp incisor teeth in the front of their mouths, much like a beaver, and eat all types of green plant life. They dig their burrows in fencerows and woodlots where they can easily sneak out into fields of young growing crops and wreak havoc. Like mini combines they choose a row of tender young soybean plants, straddle the row and eat every plant off to the ground for several feet.

We had a dog named "Silly" who was a groundhog slayin' machine. A groundhog can give a nasty bite, but Silly knew just how and where to grab them and would shake them till those giant incisor teeth rattled.

One day we heard a huge ruckus coming from the cornfield by the house. Upon investigation, it was Silly who had caught a groundhog, probably sneaking through the cornfield on its way back to the safety of its den, or so it thought. When the fight was over, Silly was victorious as usual, the groundhog was dead, and a patch of corn the size of a pickup was flattened from the fray.

Now, old man Campbell, the teenage-boy-hating neighbor across the road, had a dog named Wimpy. As I remember Wimpy looked sort of like a cross between a beagle, a basset, and a sack of potatoes. He was a good old dog, just not the sharpest knife in the drawer. This particular day, Campbell's hay was ready to bale, and, as usual, three of us neighbor boys suddenly became handier to him than sliced bread! The hay field was bordered by a creek on one side and by woods on one end, and those borders were riddled with woodchuck dens.

Empty wagons were pulled behind the baler, and when one was loaded, ol' man Campbell would stop long enough for one of us minions to unhook the loaded one, hook up to the empty wagon behind us and off we'd go again. In the middle of one such exchange, we heard the most awful wailing, screeching, and thrashing imaginable—like Beelzebub himself had come a-callin'—coming from the nearby field edge. The three of us kids ran to investigate and found Wimpy in the weeds with a big groundhog stuck-like-chuck to the end of his snout! Around and around they went, the woodchuck showing no intentions of letting go. We all knew better than to try and interrupt the festivities barehanded, so we scrambled to find something to end the brawl and save Wimpy's snout.

The back of all the hay wagons had metal "pockets" welded to them into which wooden racks could be inserted to provide something solid to stack the back row of hay bales against. One wagon happened to have just single two-by-fours in those pockets, so someone grabbed one and ran back to the brawl. After taking careful aim amidst the ball of thrashing fur, a well placed wallop across the groundhog's back dropped it to the ground and sent it diving for its burrow minus Wimpy, who raced shrieking toward the house. So ended Wimpy's close encounter with the woodchuck, and I sincerely doubt he ever saw one that close again.

Jake and the Bone Pile

My sister had an old lab named Jake, a stray as I remember it. Jake was old and a little crippled and was kind of the color of light brown gravy. Like ol' man Campbell's dog, Wimpy, Jake often seemed dumber than a bag - a- hammers, but he knew no strangers. He was big and stocky and when his tail got to waggin' his whole back end wagged. His back half would fling from side-to-side so violently I often expected something

from back there to come loose and fly across the yard! He always greeted visitors with something in his mouth, wanting to play fetch; trouble was that "something" would be a four-foot two-by-four or a tree limb of like proportions. Once his body got to waggin' with his chosen tree limb or 2x4 in his mouth, he could easily take you out with a whack across the legs. Ol' Jake's obsession took him far and wide over the farm to find just the object to carry around in his position as head greeter.

Every livestock farm, whether chickens, turkeys, hogs, sheep or cattle—like it or not—has occasional casualties from sickness or cold weather. And every livestock farm has a "bone pile," a spot somewhere in the "back 40" where carcasses can be dumped in a ravine or a briar patch as a way to discreetly dispose of them while Mother Nature and the coyotes compost them. The first year I trapped beavers in Kansas, I learned to take advantage of the bone pile on my sister's farm as a convenient way to dispose of beaver carcasses after I had removed their pelts. I had traps nearby, so every time I caught a beaver, I'd just carry the carcass with me the following morning and deposit it on the pile when I was in the neighborhood—very convenient for me.

One particularly cold morning I got a call from my sister; she sounded a little miffed, but I could tell she was on the verge of laughter even as we spoke. It seems she had looked out into the yard this cold frozen morning to find Jake playing with his usual large prize, but something looked odd about that day's trophy. So curiosity sent her into the yard to see just what he had found this time. As she approached, Jake's back end began to wag feverishly and he spun around and greeted her with a whole frozen beaver carcass from the bone pile clenched proudly in his big yap!

Yup, dogs are the epitome of unconditional love and acceptance. One minute they can seem dumber than a box of rocks, the next minute they curl up beside you in your old recliner and become your most loyal friend, despite the names you have just called them for performing certain hygiene functions in the middle of the dining room. Mutts, you gotta love 'em!

22

Ol' Stumpy

I have a love-hate relationship with squirrels, also known as limb chickens or tree bacon in our neck of the woods. They taunt our two little pups from the top of my back fence or from the roof of our neighbor's garage and work them into an absolute frenzy. They hang upside-down from their heels on the side of the tree, just out of reach and chatter away as if to say, "Come and get me, you yappy little mongrels!"

Squirrels are not to be trifled with and can give a nasty bite, but just once I wish my dumb mutts would learn to work together and snag one. Like maybe one pup could prance around the tree with a big grin on its face, clutching an acorn in its teeth, luring the little bird-feeder-vandal near the ground, while the other pup sneaks up from the other side, pounces on its back and cleans it off the side of tree. But it would be just my luck the squirrel would weigh more than the dog and instead of crumpling to the ground with the pooch on its back, it would head for the top of the tree with the pooch on its back. At that point I don't know which would be worse, the hapless hound hangin' on to end up somewhere in the treetops, or fallin' off somewhere over the middle of the yard.

Pesky as they are, I know of no other wild critter in the U.S. more pampered than the squirrel. I have to admit squirrels are fun to watch as they roll around inside those glass jar feeders. I've always wanted to catch a squirrel inside one and run out and screw the lid on before it could flee. We buy corn to feed them, and then buy feeders to hold the corn. We teach them to take peanuts from our hands, and I even heard of someone who had taught the little beggars to tap on the front door when they wanted a handout. Last year at the fair we bought a rig that suspends two ears of corn side-by-side above the ground, forcing them to jump up and hang onto the corn while they get a mouthful.

Lately a squirrel with only half a tail has become a regular at our new feeder; we've named it "Ol' Stumpy." We thought at first that Stumpy was a male, but when they hang spread-eagled from the corn with both right feet on one ear and both left on the other and spin around in the process, looking like a centerfold for Play Squirrel, it becomes fairly simple to examine them anatomically. There are no bulging body parts on Stumpy's underside so we've deemed her a girl.

We can only guess at how Stumpy lost the end of her tail. Perhaps at Stumpy's last home, some yappy little mongrel did get a piece of her, proudly wagging its tail as it showed its master nothing but the back half of Ol' Stumpy's tail. Or maybe Stumpy was one of those squirrels that someone taught to knock on the front door for a treat. We have lots of seniors in our little town, and I can see it all now: old Mrs. Dinglemire up the street who's partly deaf and mostly blind hears a tapping sound at her front door and when she opens it, there stands Ol'(Not Yet) Stumpy. Now, Ol' (Not Yet) Stumpy looks like a rat to her, so she grabs her broom and swings it at the innocent squirrel, entangling it's thick tail in the broom, so when she lifts the broom the squirrel comes with it and … well, you get the picture; somehow in the melee the little panhandler's tail gets snapped off in the door and Ol' (Not Yet) Stumpy becomes Ol' Stumpy.

I did a little research on Ol' Stumpy's tail dilemma on a website named "The Squirrel Board" (I can't make this stuff up!) It seems Ol' Stumpy's not alone and squirrel tails are made so they will "deglove" or snap off if a predator has hold of it. The jury seemed to still be out as to whether it would ever grow back and Stumpy would be whole again. The squirrel lovers on that site are out of my league. One guy said, "If you're feeding peanuts to your squirrels, make sure they are roasted…I feed mine chopped almonds because they are healthier than peanuts." (Really? Sounds like his squirrels eat better than I do.) He goes on to say, "Thanksgiving week we fed them almonds, cashews, pistachios, walnuts, chestnuts and hazelnuts for a variety." I have to admit that would make for some tasty squirrel if you roasted 'em while they were still full of nuts.

Now, even though Cousin Eddy from the National Lampoon movie "Christmas Vacation" says squirrels are high in cholesterol, they are not. Bentonville Arkansas, headquarters of Walmart, has an annual World Champion Squirrel Cook-Off that draws TV crews, executive chefs and visitors from around the globe. Their theme is "Squirrel – it's for Supper," and they offer "organic tree-to-table squirrel" in dishes like squirrel pizza and squirrel flavored ice cream. And are you aware there is actually an organization called "Squirrels Unlimited?"(SQU for short) Its mission statement reads: SQU is dedicated to the recognition and promotion of the squirrel as one of mankind's greatest gifts."

There is also a market for squirrel tails. Fishing lure manufacturer Mepps in Wisconsin actually pays for squirrel tails because they seem to work better as skirts on their fishing lures than any other product they have tried. Depending on the species of tails you send, they pay between

8 and 16 cents apiece for batches under 100, and 22 to 26 cents apiece for lots over 1000. On their website they caution "Mepps is only interested in "Recycling" tails from squirrels harvested for the table. We do not advocate taking squirrels strictly for their tails." Mepps says that when they receive the tails, members of their experienced team will grade the tails as premium, average or unusable. Sorry Stumpy, I guess you're out of luck there, too. Maybe she purposely "degloved" her own tail to keep me from being tempted!

You know, now that I've written all this about Stumpy, I feel kinda' bad for her, busted snapped-off tail and all. I mean, she's gotta' be self conscious enough already without me dissin' her like this. Now that I think about it, I haven't seen her around for awhile. Maybe she's holed up in her nest haven' little Stumpys, or maybe she got run off by the rest of the local nut munchers, or maybe she just couldn't take the shame anymore and decided to end it all by throwing herself in front of a school bus. I knew I should have gotten her counseling, and given everything people do for squirrels these days, I probably could've found that, too!

23
101 Uses for a Feral Cat

Cats of any description are fierce, efficient hunters and feral cats all the more. They do untold damage to pheasant and quail populations and kill large numbers of songbirds. By feral cats I mean cats that live totally in the wild and possibly haven't had a domestic relative for years or even generations—NOT "Fluffy" next door that rolls around at your feet and plays hide and seek with you from a paper sack.

Feral cats have become so overpopulated in some states that hunting seasons have been proposed for them, but I think I have some better ideas. For starters, how about using them for crowd control. Rioting crowds would probably react badly to snarling German Shepherds, but who's gonna notice a few fluffy cats rubbing against everyone's legs. Really long-haired ones rolled in some sort of fairy dust and turned loose to spread it through the crowd could have the demonstrators simply falling asleep where they stood. All that's needed is to pile everyone against the curbs and traffic is restored—no buildings burned, no one shot, and just look at the money saved on tear gas. Hopefully when the protestors all awoke to see how pathetic they looked on the evening news, they would just slink off into the shadows and be too ashamed to try it again. Carousing kitties could also work well as airport security, putting even the crankiest passengers at ease as they rolled around at their feet, all the while sniffing for drugs and contraband.

Feral felines would really shine in the outdoors. I envision an entire stable of them to rent out as living four-legged heating pads, available to us hunters as foot, neck and lap warmers as we sit in deer and duck blinds. I'd call my whiskered employees something like Cozy Kitties or Toasty Tabbies.

Cats always want to sleep and just naturally curl up in a ball anyway, so simply lay a pair on your boots or drape a couple across your shoulders and let nature take its course. Ditto for ice fishermen as they sit on overturned five-gallon buckets on frozen lakes. A long-haired tabby wrapped around their necks like a scarf and one laid across each boot would really help cut the chilly wind. Sure, you might be the laughing stock of the lake for awhile…until all your buddies are dancing around with icicles in their long johns, trying to get warm. Then a few extra Cozy Kitties kept in your truck would be rented out in no time, payin' you enough to stop at the seafood counter at Dillons on the way home when the fish didn't bite (yes, I say this from experience!) Football fans might also enjoy one or two cat warmers wrapped around them as they brave the elements to cheer on their favorite teams.

Winter campers would benefit doubly from a couple of Toasty Tabbies tucked into their sleeping bags. When we were kids we'd ride in grandpa's truck camper as he sped down the road on fishing trips, and the gentle rocking of the camper would put us to sleep in a heartbeat. Just imagine how fast you'd be asleep with a Cozy Kitty curled up beside you in your sleeping bag and purring like a bear in a honey factory.

Big cities always have rodent problems, so why not train my feline foot warmers for rodent control too, using some catchy name like Steve's Marvelous Mousers. I'd roll into town about dusk and start distributing the Marvelous Mousers along alleys and side streets, then return to my Airstream parked somewhere out in the 'burbs for a good night's sleep. Just before dawn the next morning little GPS units on each collar would help me find all my Mousers, which by then would probably be so full of fat little city-slicker mice that all they'd want to do is sleep anyway, making them a breeze to collect; and can you imagine how many of them would fit into cages in the back of a pickup! The biggest problems would arise after they had slept awhile and processed all those mice. I'd either have to let them out to potty and hope I could find them all again, or pull an old pickup-bed trailer behind the Airstream to use as a giant litter-box.

Despite their worthiness in the outdoors, feral cats would have their limitations. For instance, can you picture them as retrievers? Forget sending them after a downed pheasant; by the time they got into the mood, the grass would have grown a foot taller and your bird would be fertilizer.

And I'm guessin' anything water related involving swimming would be out. I suppose you could fit your feline-fetcher with a tiny flotation device, then chuck it into the lake like a life preserver and, when it had latched onto the downed duck or goose, pull them both back to shore; and good luck getting them to do that more than once!

Well, there you have just a few examples of my 101 uses for a feral cat. I see it as a win-win-deal; a few feral cats are taken out of the wild, pet lovers are happy 'cause they weren't killed, and we hunters reap the benefits. Why, I'll bet the poor misled folks at PETA would even be proud of me … hmmm, if that's my reward maybe I need to rethink this whole thing.

24

Pest Hunts

When I was sixteen, I had that all-too-common kid's disease known as "doesn't work to his potential" syndrome, so FFA (Future Farmers of America) could have stood for Famous Fruits of Arabia, Fat Farmers of Australia or Flying Felines of Argentina for all I knew. But FFA was OK in my book because we had pest hunts!

Pest hunts started in the fall and ran for a couple months. We divided into teams of four or five and for those couple months killed all the pests we could kill. Everything had a point value; starlings and blackbirds were two points each, pigeons were five and so on and so forth. It was a simple competition to see which team could accumulate the most points by the end of the time period. As proof of "capture," the heads of all birds were kept, and the tails were kept from mice, rats, 'possums and most everything else. And since all "trophies" were accumulated until the contest was over, they naturally had to be housed in the freezer. And since most folks only had one freezer back then, it was the same freezer where all the frozen meat, vegetables, and fruit were kept. Yup, more than once I remember Mom screamin' my name in capital letters when she came up with a bag full of bird heads or 'possum tails instead of the frozen corn or hamburgers she was after.

The pest hunting game plan was fairly straightforward. We were all farm kids, so mice and rats were killed as we saw them around the barn. We were also hunters and trappers so 'possums were found squashed along the road or caught in our 'coon traps, in which case we clubbed them dead instead of holding them by the tail and punting them over the fence onto the neighbor's yard like usual.

Bird hunting gigs were the trickiest. Most barns where I grew up were three or four stories tall with haylofts on each end. There was always a window high in each end of the barn with a ladder running up the inside wall to the window. One hunter would climb each ladder up to the window, turn around, and prepare to swat birds as they headed toward the opening, all the while somehow holding onto the ladder for dear life. Now, that doesn't sound all that dangerous, but here's the thing: it was all done in the dead of night.

Here's how the process worked. Our team would quietly converge on a barn around 10 p.m. or so. (Of the whole process, the "quietly" part was the toughest.) Remember this was winter, so everyone was dressed in old army jackets and mud boots, except the designated "swatters" for that night's offensive, who had to dress warmly but in clothing that fit loosely around the shoulders so as not to impede their swing once they got into place at the top of the ladders. Clubs for the battle ranged from

top-of-the-line gear like tennis or badminton rackets to more simple weapons like a scrap board with a handle nailed to it. Once the climbing swatters were inserted and in place, the rest of the militia on the floor would turn on lights and make as much noise as possible, attempting to roust any birds roosted inside, which would inevitably head for the windows, now guarded by the "swatters." Snipers (with pellet guns) would begin picking off any drowsy birds still clinging to their perches after the melee started.

Meanwhile, at the tops of the ladders, startled birds were flying into a trap, and the action could be fast and furious as flustered birds of all shapes and sizes tried to fly out the windows, and Heaven help you if one of those birds was an owl! For starters, you only had one hand available to swat as the other was rather busy holding onto an old rickety ladder that you hoped would not crumble into pieces and dump you into the hay below. These were still the days of small square bales of hay and straw, which might have been only a few feet below you or twenty feet below you, depending on how much the farmer had used already. It was still pretty dark up there and, with birds often coming at you several at a time, it was impossible to swat them all. The ones you missed either flew around, coming back for a second try, or just hit you in the face from the get-go. It was pretty cool when you clobbered one squarely, as its lifeless chassis would sail across the barn, leaving a big poof of feathers in the air. In the midst of the assault it could be raining dead bird carcasses down on the floor and it wasn't out of the question to get whacked up side the noggin with the corpse of a deceased pigeon or starling if you were down there. We always tried to make sure the guys on the ground with the pellet guns were the most even-tempered of the group, thereby lessening the chance that one of the swatters would get shot in the butt for inadvertently beaning someone with a bird cadaver.

After all forms of pest-life seemed to be vanquished from a barn, out came the flashlights and it was time to collect the spoils. We'd yank off all the bird's heads, stuff em' into a bag and go on down the road to the next barn, leaving the neighborhood barn cats quite a feast indeed for allowing us to invade their territory.

How many times have you looked back upon crazy things you did as a kid and wondered how in blazes you ever survived past the age of nine? Every time I drive past a tall barn with windows in each end, I stare up at the windows and ask myself "Did we really used to do that?" Well, I've lived well past the age of nine and another part of me has to wonder if the world would be a better place today if we just had more pest hunts.

25

Rattlesnake Relocation Project

It was a small story a few years ago on the back page of the local Sunday paper. It read "Rattlesnake relocation project comes to an end." Now, any outdoor writer worth his or her summer sausage would instantly be drawn to headlines like that, and here's the story as I understand it. Incidentally, all names have been changed to protect participants in this project from residents of this town, who might just be hearing about this for the first time.

In the spring of 2007, Lenexa, Kansas residents began spotting an ever increasing number of rattlesnakes in some neighborhoods. While checking on the construction site for a never-built Target store, the city construction inspector discovered numerous rattlesnakes lying around the site. It was determined that a large rattlesnake den existed somewhere under a big pile of construction rubble there. To Dr. WWYT (short for What Were You Thinking) biology professor at a major out-of-state university, this seemed like the perfect opportunity to test a new conservation model; the attempted relocation of as many snakes as possible from a single population, in hopes they would establish their same population somewhere else. Around-the-clock "snake watches" were established at the den, and over the next two or three weeks, Dr. WWYT and a host of her students and other volunteers caught 35 timber rattlesnakes, implanted them with radio transmitters to permit their being tracked and deposited them at another suitable den site some miles away at a "top-secret" location.

Now, I'm more "snake-friendly" than most, but you just don't rescue rattlesnakes! You rescue Lassie or Timmy when they fall into the well. You rescue a kitten when it gets its head stuck in an empty salmon can.

You rescue a calf when the stupid thing gets caught in a gate. Heck, a guy on the news just lately even rescued a half-drowned prairie dog from his swimmin' pool, but you just don't rescue rattlesnakes! They probably even thought they were doin' the snakes a favor by takin' them out of the 'hood.

I'll never forget years ago when some bleeding-heart group wanted to remove prairie dogs from a construction site in Hutchinson, Kansas. They went to great lengths to have them sucked up and unceremoniously blown into a big padded truck, then proudly deposited them at Quivera National Wildlife Refuge. They found out later that the badgers ate them all (and probably thanked the group for ordering carry-out.) Yep, they did them quite a favor! The Lenexa rattlers pretty much had it made where they were. The worst they probably encountered were angry little old ladies with garden hoes or yappy little dogs. But their new "top-secret" home was probably somewhere out in the country where every farmer and rancher they came across would simply blow their heads off with a twelve gauge and think nothing of it; yep what a fine new home!

I spoke with the good DR. WWYT on the phone, and the opening conversation went something like this: "Doc, I'm pretty snake-friendly. I've captured my share of bull and rat snakes and turned them loose at the river or someplace where they were less likely to lose their heads, so to speak. But I gotta tell ya if I ever found a rattler crawling across my lawn, it would certainly join its deceased ancestors. So why on God's green earth would you relocate an entire den of rattlesnakes?"

Her answer was two-fold: first of all it seems that extreme eastern Kansas is probably the western most boundary of the timber rattlesnake in the U.S. and since their numbers are sparse, the Kansas Dept of Wildlife and Parks and Tourism (KDWPT) has designated them as what is known as a SINC species, which stands for Species In Need of Conservation. Because of this, timber rattlesnakes can legally be killed in Kansas ONLY if they directly threaten your safety, not just because they happen to have rattles on their tails. She calls them "the puppy dogs of the rattlesnake world," and says a timber rattler's first line of defense is to blend in rather than coil or strike, as they opt to save that energy for hunting. Secondly, she says that those snakes have likely been there for years, possibly even

before the area was built up, meaning that we humans encroached on their territory.

OK, let me get this straight, I can't kill a timber rattlesnake in Kansas unless I feel my safety is threatened, and we're going to play "the snakes were here before we were" card? Let me ask you, when's the last time you were surprised by a rattlesnake in the wild and did not feel your safety was threatened? And shame on you if you didn't stop to check your snake identification guide before lopping the critter into pieces. I dare say the coyotes and cockroaches were probably here WAY before we were, but that doesn't seem to have influenced how we greet them. As for the "puppy dogs of the rattlesnake world" comment, I know what she's trying to say, but somehow her comparison doesn't work for me. If it won't curl up on my lap and let me scratch its ears, I'm sorry, but I just can't call it a puppy dog.

The newspaper article goes on to say that a few litters of young were born during the relocation process, and the students even went so far as to name several of the adult snakes. The largest caught was just under four and half feet long, weighed two pounds or so and was thought to be 20 to 25 years old. He was named Abuelo, Spanish for grandfather.

I can see it all now: there's Abuelo propped up beside a campfire, his crutches lying beside him and his spectacles balanced precariously across his wrinkled old snout. The forked tongue that once flicked crisply in and out as he constantly tested his surroundings now hangs limp and nearly useless out of one corner of his mouth. His once needle-sharp fangs now seem almost in his way as he speaks with a slight lisp to the young timber rattlers gathered around him. He tells them of the legendary Dr. WWYT, who years ago banished them from a land of milk and honey where they had true freedom and sent them to this land they inhabit today—a land where the humans all carry giant thunder sticks that belch fire and smoke and cleanly sever their heads. He tells them how he yearns for the old country with its harmless little old ladies and yappy dogs. But he also warns them that they must all carry on the traditions that have earned them the reputation of puppy dogs of the rattlesnake world. All the younglings are silent and pensive as Abuelo slinks away to his den.

Like I said, I'm more snake-friendly than most and I'll even go out of my way to ignore or even relocate a rat or bull snake because of all the rodents they eat. But I just won't relocate a rattlesnake; unless of course it slowly slithers by on crutches and peers pleadingly at me through spectacles propped up on a wrinkled old snout…or maybe not even then!

26

Sometimes Life Just Stinks

I don't know whether or not it says something about my personality, but I seem to be drawn to unfortunate skunk encounters like a moth is drawn to a flame. I've even considered inventing a substance that I could dip myself in like a Pronto Pup wiener, then simply step out of and leave in the woods, skunk stink and all, if I happen to get sprayed. I could call it Skunk-Proof Batter or maybe Stench-Glaze. I'll let you know how that goes.

Anyway, one particular morning last year I went to check several bobcat traps I had a few miles west of town. The traps had been there long enough, and it was time to move them. A busy day was planned, so I got an early start in case hiccups occurred in getting the traps. You would think by now I would have completely removed the words "if," "in-case," and "what-if" from my vocabulary, because it's never a matter of "if" something will happen to me, it's only a matter of when.

I was ahead of schedule when I rolled into the last stop. "A few minutes here, then home to a hot breakfast," I told myself. One of the traps was a cage trap, slid back into a pile of branches with a goose carcass as bait, and I could see that the cage door was closed. From my vantage point, branches blocked my view of the entire cage, but what appeared to be a raccoon rustled around in the trap. I grabbed the handgun and headed for the cage, but suddenly I could see that the coon had a couple white stripes down its back. Chills went down my spine and I suddenly developed the nervous tick that usually precedes my doing something really stupid. "Great," I thought. "Just what I didn't want to see this morning."

Now I remembered an incident a couple years back where I had a skunk caught in a cage trap. That trap was much bigger than this one, so as the skunk put on an acrobatics show climbing and swinging around at the back of the cage, I was able to get close enough to somehow open the door and prop it open with a stick. That was one of the dumber things I have ever done in my life, but the skunk eventually left without incident.

This trap was much smaller, but the morning had been going so well, I guess I figured nothing could go wrong. It's at this point that common sense usually flees from my mind like rats from a sinking ship. This is also the point where I would dip myself in the vat of Skunk-Proof Batter in the back of my pickup. Anyway, I crept up to the trap, quietly talking to the critter as I walked. Skunks are actually pretty laid back, especially if the container is covered and you go about things slowly and quietly. Besides, as long as the thing kept its butt pointed the other way, there was no way if could spray me, right?

Just as I knelt down, the skunk charged the door, a maneuver they often use in an attempt to scare you away before they resort to spraying. I wanted to run, but a warm, wet, sticky feeling in the seat of my pants made it uncomfortable to even move. So there I was, on my hands and knees face-to-face with Pepe Le Pew himself, when it dawned on me that the little blighter had not turned its butt toward me in an effort to end my life, but in fact had backed into the rear of the cage again.

Summoning my courage and forcing common sense even farther from my being, I once again got as close as I thought I dared, and tried

gingerly raising the two steel rings that held the door shut, so I could quickly prop the door open and skedaddle. Then it happened... I heard a sort of whooshing, squirting sound, felt something hit my face and the scrambled eggs and bacon I could almost taste awaiting me at home suddenly reeked of skunk! I do solemnly swear, cross my heart and hope to spit that a skunk's butt DOES NOT have to be facing you to spray you because those beady little demon eyes never left mine during the entire assault. They can spray over their back and in about any old direction they choose.

I jumped and ran like I was going to outrun the stench or something. I wiped a couple droplets from my glasses and started peeling outer clothing that might have been hit. I grabbed the handgun and ended the little beggar's career. Then I made the phone call every hunter's wife dreads; "Honey, I just got sprayed by a skunk!"

I did a piece on skunks some years ago and my research then told me that the old tomato juice cure just doesn't work, but rather leaves you smelling like tomato juice AND skunk. Joyce found a tried-and-true cure that really does work, and she promised to have some ready when I arrived. Mix together one quart hydrogen peroxide, one quarter cup baking soda and one to two teaspoons dish soap (not laundry detergent.) Wipe down your entire body and everything else that got sprayed and then rinse. A warning, as clothing cleaned with this solution may discolor, and you may have to wash your hair a couple times—or it might cause your hair to fall out along with some of your teeth.

So I drove home in my stocking feet with the windows down. I thought seriously about stripping down to my skivvies, but sure-as-the-world a brake light would be out or something and I'd get stopped. I walked through the backyard and onto the deck where two hands strongly resembling those of my loving wife protruded from the back door. One hand held a bowl of the magic "skunk-be-gone" while the other held a bath towel and pointed toward the workshop in the back, which could easily have become my new home if that stuff hadn't worked.

I learned several things that day. First, it's never too late for things to go wrong. Secondly, it's good to know there is something that will actually remove skunk odor, and lastly, I'll never again attempt to do a skunk a favor!

27

The Great Coon Bait Caper

When it comes to eating habits, raccoons are a lot like teenage boys; they'll eat anything that smells good, and a lot of things that don't. Common home-grown coon baits are marshmallows, jelly beans, peanut butter, barbeque sauce, maple syrup and cream corn. There are people raking in the dough selling custom baked pet treats, so one year after the Kansas Fur Harvesters convention, I opened the Gilliland Coon Bait Test Kitchen, intent on dazzling the trapping world with my coon bait creations.

First order of business was to put on my lab coat and hair and beard net. My brother runs the R&D department at a brand-name dog-food plant and has to wear hair and beard nets to guard against getting hair in the dog food, so I thought it only right that I guard against hair in my raccoon bait!

I needed some early success, so for my first creation I used a jar of product I bought at the convention. The jar contains all the flavors and smells the seller uses in his raccoon bait; you merely add the jar contents to one pound of dog or cat food. I marched into my woodworking-shop-turned-test-kitchen with a bag of Walmart's cheapest cat food under my arm. In a monstrous Ziploc storage bag I mixed the cat food and the powder in the jar, which smelled sweet and yummy like butterscotch. The whole shop (I mean test kitchen) smelled like butterscotch for three days. It's good I'm not a sleepwalker; I probably would have awakened late that night and found myself eating a bowl of it with milk.

For my second creation I wanted to try a recipe I found on the all-wise, all-knowing internet. The base for this recipe was commercial pond fish food. At the recent trapper's convention, I'd been warned repeatedly not to use commercial fish food as it quickly deteriorates into mush when it gets damp. I poured my commercial fish food into a one-gallon ice cream bucket (the surest way to goad me into trying something is to warn me repeatedly against it) which I placed on the step going into the garage. When I returned a while later, there sat an empty ice cream bucket on the step. It suddenly dawned on me that the bucket was exactly like the one that holds the dog food in the pantry for our little wiener dog, Lucy. My wife saw the bucket of fish food on the step, thought it was nice of me to refill Lucy's dog food bucket and promptly fed her a heaping bowl of commercial pond fish food! No harm done, the ingredients are probably not much different than those in dog food anyway, but now not only does Lucy love to get a bath, I have to chase her around the sink as she keeps swimming away from me!

With a Ziploc bag of the fish food and various other ingredients, I entered the SATELLITE test kitchen, a.k.a. my wife's real kitchen. This was still a test, so I used just a small amount of the fish pellets, then added mini-marshmallows, molasses and vanilla according to the recipe. I mixed

it all together and sealed the bag. It smelled like my grandmother's ginger cookies times ten, but looked like it had already been eaten once. In my defense, at least it was a palatable kitcheny smell and didn't reek of rotten eggs or dirty gym socks like many trapping baits.

I let the concoction marinate for a few days, then decided it was not exactly what a finicky, man-of-the-world raccoon might want to smear all over his face. I found a bulk food store and came home with butterscotch oil, peppermint oil and anise oil, all of which, by the way are oft-used ingredients in commercially made raccoon bait.

Anise oil smells like black licorice and I decided to play with it first. I opened the jar of the afore-mentioned gingerbread smelling goo and tore off a softball-sized chunk, put it into its own container and began adding the anise. My drum beats to the tune that "More is always better," so I dumped every last drop from the three tiny bottles into the goo and mixed it as best I could. It was soft and pliable all right but mixing it was like trying to stir something into a volleyball. When I finished, it smelled like an explosion at a black licorice factory, but looked like a bowl of cow brains.

Next was the butterscotch oil. I had only two little bottles of it, so again I ripped off a chunk of the gingerbread goo and added the oil. It actually smelled yummy, like a combination of grandma's cookies and Werther's candies, but looked no different than the first.

Last but not least was the peppermint oil. Again I pried off a lump of the goo and added the peppermint. I intentionally took a big whiff of the oils before adding them to the mix, and the peppermint was the sharpest of the three. It was sweet like peppermint, but almost overpowering. When finally mixed, this last attempt smelled like wonderful sweet wedding mints, but still looked like cow brains.

I'm embarrassed to say that the test kitchen experiments were the highlight of this project. The only catch made with my experimental offerings was a 'possum—understandable I guess, using bait that looks like cow brains. Anyway, it all made for a good story and taught me a lesson. No, it didn't; I'm sure I'll try it all again next year!

28

The Midnight Perils of Hunting Frogs

The black, oozy, mire that called itself the bottom of the pond allowed me to take the step I desired, but it held onto the boot and my foot took the step alone! The boots were full chest waders strapped across my shoulders so I was never going to step completely free of them, but now my foot had pulled out of the "foot" part of the boot and I was left standing in two feet of mucky pond water trying to push my foot back down into the boot, which by now had twisted around under me. My balance is horrible anyway, so there I stood in the pitch darkness, guided only by the two flashlight beams of me and my frog hunting partner, trying to "right my ship" before I toppled headfirst into the deep. Finally, mission accomplished, I briefly sat down on the bank to get things adjusted and to convince myself I would probably not drown tonight. Then off we went again.

"Paul Revere's Ride" by Henry Wadsworth Longfellow begins "Listen my children and you shall hear of the midnight ride of Paul Revere." All my frog hunting tales should begin "Listen my readers whilst' I blog 'bout the midnight perils of hunting frogs." For me, the number one inconvenience in nighttime frog hunting is the mucky bottom of most ponds, combined with submerged sticks and tree limbs that can't be seen. I can spray for the skeeters', there is no limit to the size of flashlight I can buy to light-up the night around me, but there is no "app" on my phone to turn a mucky pond bottom to sand and rid it of hidden tree limbs, which I'm convinced take on human form after dark and grab my ankles to topple me face-first into the drink.

Now, I'm not much of a team sports player, but frog huntin' the way we used to do it came terribly close to being a team sport. Half the fun of our frog hunts was just being there with our buddies, and the anticipation of what would go wrong. Whenever we went on any kind of foray after dark, the vehicle ended up broken down, stuck in the snow or mud or in the ditch, so the more passengers in the car to help extract us from our predicament the better. Our transportation needs were simple; four wheels, two seats and something that already smelled as badly as we would when the night was over, which was easily accomplished because that perfectly described all our vehicles.

Near our home in central Ohio was a farm with two ponds, one on each side of the main highway that passed our homestead. One memorable frog hunt took place at these ponds late on a hot steamy Ohio night. I've always questioned the landowner's sanity for allowing us there unsupervised; I can only surmise he hoped we'd all drown and never bother him again. Anyway, Ralph (my rabbit hunting partner) and his brother Mike, Terry and I, all piled into Terry's old beater of a car, intent upon harvesting a "mess" of tasty frog legs from these ponds. Terry's ride was chosen because it easily met the above transportation criteria, plus the radio worked.

We had found the best "froggin" attire to be old jeans, and worn-out sneakers, which we wore all the time anyway. Hip boots or waders sound good, but inevitably you'd end up horizontal in the pond before the night was done, and once waders fill with water, it's like wearing a fifty gallon barrel around each leg. (Yes, I know this from experience.)

There are several legal ways to harvest frogs. We chose "gigs"—small pitchfork shaped spears used on the ends of long bamboo poles. These work quite well on frogs, but in the dark you soon learned to keep a good distance between you and the guy behind you, as an errant gig to the butt made the evening go by really slowly! A bright flashlight was shone at the frog's eyes, blinding them long enough to be speared with the gig. Armed with frog gigs, flashlights and gunnysacks to hold our catch, and clad in ragged jeans and worn out sneakers, we must have looked like characters from the movie "Huck Finn meets the Grim Reaper."

The night was soon filled with the deep throbbing "harum" sounds of bullfrogs. As I remember, we split up to conquer the two ponds faster. We slogged slowly along the banks as quietly as possible, each step threatening to suck us deeper into the oozy muck that smelled like rotten eggs.

(I was always suspicious that it wasn't really the mud that smelled like rotten eggs.) We stalked along, knee deep in the water, until the glistening skin or gleaming beady eyes of a frog appeared in the beam of the flashlight. The trick was to slowly lower the spear as close to the frog as possible before striking, and hold the light in their eyes to keep them "dazzled," all the while using Jedi mind games to persuade the frog to give itself up. While this anchored the frog so we could retrieve it, it usually didn't kill it, so we soon had bags full of squirming amphibians trying to swim away from the frying pan.

We got lots of frogs that night and decided to clean them at my place on the way home. We had a big circular driveway with a security light on a tall pole in the middle. An empty hay wagon pulled under the light made the perfect butchering table, and we were soon at it. As gunnysacks were emptied, squirming frogs went everywhere and we boisterously went to work. At one point I remember mom hollering out the upstairs window for us to be quiet: I don't know what her problem was, it was only 2 AM! We removed the legs, then skinned them much like skinning a catfish, leaving the big flipper feet attached. They fry up white, sweet and tender, and NO, they do not taste just like chicken!

Half the fun of a frog hunt, besides the obvious frog-leg lunch is watching the legs as they fry. In the hot grease, the thick meaty pieces quiver and tremble as if they were still alive, much to the chagrin of anyone trying frog legs for the first time. I remember one particular frog-leg feast attended by one of my buddy's girlfriends who had never tasted frog legs before, and was very apprehensive about ever doing so, let alone with us. I was frying and, when she was out of the room, I found one especially big set of legs and propped them up on the edge of the skillet with the legs crossed, just as if they had climbed out of the skillet and were resting there. I don't know who was madder at me, she at the sight of them or my buddy because I had done it!

These days I hardly ever hunt frogs anymore. Maybe because it's not as much fun as it used to be slogging around in some farm pond after dark. Maybe it's because no one else will go with me because they all feel the same as I do about slogging around in some farm pond after dark. Whatever the reason, I still get to enjoy an occasional mess of frog legs, and they still taste as sweet and tender as they did 50 years ago.

29

The Thrill of Road Kill

There have been a couple distinct phases, (for lack of a better term) in the nearly twenty-two year marriage to my understanding and most tolerant wife, Joyce. For this discourse I'll call those phases pre-hunting and post-hunting. When we met, she had never hunted in her life, nor did she care to. Not that she was against it; she'd just grown up in a non-hunting family and therefore had no understanding of its fulfilling effect on one's life. Now, in our post-hunting days, she understands and has harvested Kansas deer and turkeys as well as accompanied me on my trapline.

That change also brought an about-face on how she feels about and deals with road-killed critters (referred to from here-on-out as "road kill.") Pre-hunting days would see her turn her head the other way and almost cower in the pickup seat as we approached and passed every unfortunate, flattened vulture hors d'oeuvre. Now in the post-hunting era, however, she is usually the first to spot an approaching road-kill, oft craning her neck and nearly crawling up onto the dashboard if necessary to correctly identify the hapless, deceased beast as we whiz past. In fact, on trips we often keep a running count of how many road-killed varmints we see of each species, much like normal kids keep track of license plates. I have even considered fabricating a little abacus of sorts to mount on the dash for just that purpose. It would have rows of tiny pegs, each representing a different animal. We would add washers to the pegs, or maybe animal crackers with holes drilled in them, to keep count.

Once on a trip to southwestern Kansas, we even stopped to inspect a dead porcupine we came across along a country road. Feeling the need for proof positive of our find, (and just because the things are weird) we gingerly plucked a sandwich bag full of quills and cut off its tail and one hind foot to take with us. When we left, the poor thing looked as though it had been the victim of some sort of bizarre satanic ritual.

Considering the agendas of certain conniving politicians who would like nothing better than to (attempt) to take my guns away, or at very least, close all hunting seasons, I sometimes plan in my mind what I'll do if the day ever arrives when the only LEGAL way for me to continue eating wild game will be to harvest road-kill. I would become a "Road-Kill Griller" in the purest sense of the phrase, and I'm bettin' there are bunches more of you out there that are afraid to come forward.

Most things would be different in the life of a road-kill griller: for starters, the grilling utensils. Your spatula would become a flat ended shovel, preferably the short handled kind with the "D" shaped handle, allowing you to put maximum power behind your spatula when scraping meals from the asphalt. The fork normally used to turn steaks on the grill would become a pitchfork or potato fork, anything capable of holding your find while removing gravel with the shovel/spatula.

Timing for harvesting road-killed meals would be an important issue. The five-second rule would become the five-day rule. You would want to either get to a kill while it's fresh, or wait until it became jerky or pemmican. Beating vultures, crows and coyotes to a fresh kill would be a real challenge in our neck of the woods.

Cooking road-kill would be a whole new learning experience in itself and should definitely be done outside. The hotter the fire, the better to quickly burn off hair and sterilize your meal.

Concerning recipes, you might as well plan to toss all your favorites and start anew. I'll list a few examples: The rare find of a chicken that could once have become chicken Tetrazzini, would now be chicken flattened by machinery. The closest you'd ever get to potatoes au gratin would be opossum smells rotten. The Internet fairly teems with road-kill recipes free for the reading. A few of my favorite main dishes would be skunk skillet stew, shake'n bake snake, rack of raccoon, pavement possum and too-slow doe. Side dishes would include square of hare, fork of stork and bowl of mole.

If you were to suddenly become unemployed, I'm quite sure a good living could be had by fixing up your old camping trailer and following

the state fair or carnival circuit, peddling road-kill on a stick. It wouldn't matter what species it is; just cut it into chunks, skewer it with a stick, slather it in some sort of batter and fry it up in old French-fry grease. If you didn't tell customers what it is, I'm sure they'd think it tasted just like chicken.

The driving habits of a true road-kill griller would be changed forever. While we'd once have avoided hitting critters on the roadway at all costs, especially deer, we now would strive to hit every critter possible, especially deer. I can see where big money could be made on the invention of a snow-plow-shaped rig that, when bolted to the front of your pickup, would scoop up small and medium sized creatures as they're hit and, at just the right speed, catapult them over the cab and into the pickup bed where they'd lie stunned until you could pull off the road and finish the job with a ball bat. No Hunting signs would become No Gleaning signs, and turf wars might break out as we all tried to protect our favorite back roads, swamps and river bridges where road-kill often abounds.

Now, in the style of Jeff Foxworthy, allow me to offer some criteria to help you decide whether or not you have the propensity to become a true road-kill griller.

If you have taught your kids to count road-killed raccoons rather than Volkswagen "slug-bugs" on a trip, you could easily become a road-kill griller.

If, after failing to fill your tag for the season, you drive your pickup off the road, across the ditch, and through a field of standing corn attempting to run down a deer, you probably have the makin's of a road-kill griller.

And finally, if you smell only the savory essence of skunk skillet stew each time a skunk sprays your favorite coonhound, you're probably already a true road-kill griller!

*Note: no animals were actually road-killed for the writing of this story.

30

The Road Kill Game

My wife has a fascination with identifying road-killed critters, so in an attempt to pad our retirement nest egg (which I believe long ago tumbled from the nest and splattered on the ground) we decided to invent and market a family-friendly game to help everyone endure those awful road trips that are usually punctuated by exclamations of "Don't make me stop this car!" or "You just wait till we get home!" It's a game of skill where players have to spot and correctly identify flattened, splattered and smeared, road-killed animal carcasses seen along the road. Welcome to the game of Road Kill Skills!

The rules of the game are really quite simple: a point value is assigned to all manner of animal carcasses, and the first player to spot and identify the carcass gets the points. The game begins when the vehicle leaves the driveway, allowing less skilled players to accumulate quick points for spotting easily seen casualties on city streets or in your driveway. We're still tweaking the rules, so I'm not sure how something will score that you run over as you exit the driveway. If it's the neighbor's cat or a friendly neighborhood squirrel, it may be a deduction; after all we're not monsters! Points are assigned according to a very scientific set of parameters, and the person riding shotgun will be the judge and have final say in any and all appeals.

The point values all depend on the degree of difficulty. In the Olympics, the diver who merely manages to enter the water headfirst without doing a belly-flop will score fewer points than the diver who twists and summersaults in every conceivable direction while texting a greeting to their mother on the way down. So it is with points in the

Road Kill Skills game; the more easily identifiable the carcass, the fewer the points. Several factors should be considered when determining point values per carcass.

First determining factor will be the size of the carcass: the smaller the carcass, the more points it will be worth. For example, a large carcass of a Holstein cow will garner the player far fewer points than that of a possum or a squirrel because the bulk of the Holstein cadaver will make it much easier to identify. That brings us to the second determining factor: the condition of the deceased. The better condition of the remains, the fewer the points. Again, an intact deer corpse not yet gnawed by coyotes will score far fewer points than that of a rabbit that's in several pieces strewn along the highway. That brings us to easily identifiable markings. Bodies of skunks and raccoons which have tell-tale markings (or scents), no matter their condition, will be worth fewer points than their flattened plain-looking cousins, like rabbits and possums, simply because they should be a slam-dunk to identify even by the novice city-slicker. As a side note here, in the case of a skunk you can award bonus points to the first "smeller."

In the real estate world, it's all about Location, Location, Location, and another important factor determining point value of roadside carrion should be the body's location. During the course of the game, you will probably travel a mix of four-lane highways, single-lane blacktop roads and gravel side roads. Those will be accompanied by an assortment of mown, manicured median strips between four-lane highways and both deep and shallow ditches along single-lane roads. In accordance with the criteria above, the harder roadside remains are to spot, the more points they are worth. For example, a bloated whitetail deer carcass lying in the neatly trimmed median between freeway lanes will be much easier to see than the cadaver of some poor flattened muskrat lying in a bed of cattails deep in a roadside ditch. Therefore, the hapless deceased muskrat, being much harder to see, will be worth more points.

While discussing points for location of the carcass, perhaps a special category should be added to address point values of critters actually run down during the course of the game by the vehicle in which one is riding. Although drivers are not encouraged to participate while they drive, I'm of the opinion they should receive gratuity points if they run over a critter during the game and can correctly identify what they hit. Again, the smaller the varmint, the more points it should be worth. East-side rules can apply here, as every situation will be different. For instance, if the driver has to back up to see what was hit, it might be seen as a deduction. But if something is actually run over while backing up to see what was hit, it could mean double bonus points. If the driver has to stop and scrape the corpse off the vehicle's grill, remove it from the hood or pry it from beneath the car, maybe the rules should automatically suspend the match while the driver calls the insurance company.

The "location" category would not be complete without awarding points for the remains of road-killed carrion still on the road. Here the rules can get fuzzy; until now, the larger the body, the fewer the points. But it seems only fitting to award bonus points for large carcasses still on the roadway, as the driver might have to execute some Dale Earnhardt NASCAR maneuvers to keep from running over them. And if the players in the car are able to correctly identify the remains while careening down the road like passengers in a tilt-a-whirl gondola, their skills should be aptly rewarded. A word of warning to players here: please don't ever remove your seatbelts during the game, as we must stress safety at all times! Bear in mind all the above suggestions are for matches played during daylight hours, so points awarded to participants after dark should be increased appropriately.

Nothing says family vacation fun like an enjoyable game to pass the time while in the car, and a lively game of Road Kill Skills might just be the ticket. Come up with your own point values, develop your own categories and rules, or simply follow the suggestions above. Levels of achievement can be set just like in Candy Crush. Points can be redeemed for Dairy Queen treats, McDonald's cheeseburgers or for those with stronger stomachs, beef jerky at gas-station stops. What a great way for the entire family to get off the couch and enjoy the great outdoors!

31

'Twas the Night before Christmas

'Twas the night before Christmas and all through the house
Not a creature was stirring EXCEPT that darn mouse.
It chewed and it rustled, so to honor my spouse
I set out some traps for that darn pesky mouse.

We don't have a chimney, or mantle or poker
And the nearest we own to a fireplace is a smoker.
Our stockings were all holey and strewn under the bed
So our old hunting boots hung by the smoker instead.

Our puppy was nestled all snug in her bed
Under the laundry room table with her stuffed toy named Fred.
She quivered and whimpered; to watch her was funny
As she dreamed she would finally corral that ol' bunny.

My PJs were long johns, all cozy and white
And I crawled into bed and turned out the light.
Deer season had ended with no deer in the shed
So visions of deer jerky danced in my head.

My wife lay beside me in jammies of red.
She was already dreaming of Claus and his sled
When out in the drive there arose such a ruckus
 I sprang from my bed to see what had struck us.

I should have known not to "spring" from my bed
Cause I busted my big toe and clobbered my head.

As I limped up the hallway I grabbed my deer rifle
I'd show them I was someone with whom not to trifle!

I peered out the window and what did I see?
Why, old Santa himself, alive as could be
And there stood old Rudolf in all of his glory,
With his nose shining brightly just like in the story.

But all I could see was his head on my wall
With that bright red nose twinkling to brighten my hall.
His rack was enormous, at least twenty points;
The thought of its score made me weak in my joints.

I wanted that rack, whether legal or not,
So I eased out the door to line up my shot.
I clicked off the safety and steadied myself
So I wouldn't endanger the Jolly Old Elf.

Now, remember those traps I'd set out before?
Well, there happened to be one right by the door.
While I tried to be sneaky so no one would know
That trap clamped its jaws around my sore big toe.

I jerked on the trigger and the shot went astray
And ended up lodged in the front of the sleigh.
The reindeer all spooked and yanked on the sled
Dumping St. Nick on the floor on his head.

They shot out the drive as slick as a whistle
And away they all flew like the down of a thistle.
But I heard him exclaim as they drove out of sight,
"Rudolph you blockhead; no more deer hunters tonight!"

I couldn't believe that in front of my house
I'd almost shot Santa because of that mouse.
At least Rudolph's safe, I thought with a smile,
But I bet this means coal in my boot for a while.

*Note: the events depicted above DO NOT reflect the ethics of the author. No reindeer were harmed in the telling of this story.

32

Wacky Warnings

Somewhere on my lengthy list of unanswered questions is the query that asks "Just how far will we go to protect ourselves from ourselves?" Don't get me wrong, there are some very necessary warnings out there, like huge letters on a tank of gasoline that read "FLAMMABLE," or flags that tell us "Road Work Ahead." But for every good and reasonable warning are a dozen other absolutely wacky warnings that leave me shaking my head.

The thing to remember about wacky warnings is that they got there because someone, somewhere, actually did what the warnings tell you not to do. So someone, somewhere, tried eating that deodorant stick before the warning "Do Not Ingest" was put there. The same goes for the words "For External Use Only" and I'll leave that to your imagination. I'm convinced the need for most wacky warnings come about as dares, and are preceded by those four, infamous little words, "Here, Hold My Beer."

The outdoor industry is not immune to wacky warnings and offers plenty of products that bear them. The owner's manual for a new gun I bought says, "Appropriate use for this firearm means using your firearm for legal purposes." So evidently, criminals using guns to commit crimes haven't read the owner's manual first? "Always keep fingers and other body parts away from the muzzle" is another firearm warning. I already know there's a hole in the end of the barrel where that thing comes out, oh now what's it called…oh ya, the bullet, so I shouldn't have to feel around there with my finger to find it, and I can't imagine what other body parts the warning means. The manual for my crossbow tells me "Always THINK before you shoot." Now, why'd they have to go and open that can-o'-worms?

And speaking of worms, I found "Not for human consumption" on all fish bait, whether artificially made from who-knows-what, or catfish stink bait made from blood, liver and other organic stuff. Now, I may have had this fishin' thing wrong all along. I've always thought the goal was to use the bait to catch fish to take home and eat, not to sit in the boat and eat the bait. Part of the fun of fishing for me has always been takin' along a nice picnic lunch or at least snacks. I really can't picture myself taking a loaf of bread and making sandwiches by spreading slices of bread with stinky catfish bait.

On one particular brand of catfish stink bait, I found the warning "Beware, dogs love this stuff." Not sure I'd have put that on the jar if my goal was to sell that bait to fishermen to actually catch fish. And I'm not sure why I should "Beware" that my dog might love it. Should I "Beware" because all my expensive bait might disappear, and show up later that night as chunks all over the couch that now smell worse than the bait, or because the dog could grow fins and swim away down the river?

One particular artificial bait made by the Berkley Company looks like crayfish packed in a pouch of liquid of some sort. It's called "Gulp Alive" and the warning reads "Looks alive, Feels alive, Tastes alive; not for human consumption." Now, to a good-ol' boy out for a relaxing day on the water, that's like dealing him all four aces and asking him not to play them! A package of Mister Twister rubber worms offered the warning "Do not use as a toy for children." Sounds like something the city-slicker uncle might give a little niece or nephew for Christmas along with hot pads and a salad shooter.

I checked the archery department of the local sporting-goods store and found a warning on all the arrows that read "Caution, razor-sharp blades." Now, I don't know who else besides bow hunters would buy those arrows, but I'm pretty sure the bow hunters I know all count on those arrows being razor sharp or they would not be buying them. To me that's like telling me "Caution, this water is wet." I also found toy arrows with suction cups on the end sporting a warning "Recommended for target shooting only." Well that takes all the fun out of it. I know if I'd gotten arrows like that when I was a kid, the dog, the cat and maybe even grandma would be strollin' around with arrows hangin' off them.

Perhaps the product I was most surprised to find warnings on were the little hand, foot and toe warmers that you stick inside your gloves or boots. The warning read "Caution, for external use only. Do not allow contents to contact eyes or mouth." OK, I'll take the high road here with the "external use only" warning and tell you how shocked I am that I can't eat hand warmers! Yes, there have been a few times while sitting in a deer blind when I've neglected to pack a snack and wished I had just a little something to nibble on, but I can honestly say I've never considered chomping on my hand or foot warmers. As for the rest of the warning, I can't remember the last time my mouth or eyes got cold and I considered putting a hand or foot warmer on them.

On canisters of black powder used for muzzle-loading guns, I found this odd warning: "Caution, do not eat, drink or smoke around this product." Now, a warning against smoking anywhere near gunpowder is one of those things that should never have to be said, but why not eat or drink around black powder? I have to remind myself again that these warnings usually come about because of some actual event. Maybe someone somewhere was once enjoying a sandwich while loading their muzzleloader, unknowingly ingested some black powder from the air along with the sandwich, and the next morning while completing their morning constitutional blew the outhouse into the next county.

All right, the time has come for my absolute favorite wacky warning found on a spray can of bear-attack deterrent. Toward the end of the somewhat lengthy warning were these words of wisdom "Do not seek out encounters with bears or intentionally provoke them." Sage advice no doubt, but let's think this through. Who among us in possession of a new toy of some sort has not tried it out immediately after removing it from the packaging? After all, we want to know if that rifle is accurate at 1000 yards like they said, or if that new bow will actually nail a deer at 50 yards. I mean if I'm going to have confidence in my new bear-attack deterrent, I need to test it. And spraying my wife's cat or the neighbor's Herford bull will probably not garner the desired results. Luckily, where I live I couldn't find a bear to "intentionally seek out an encounter with" if I wanted to, so if I get the notion to buy spray cans of bear-attack deterrent for next year's stocking stuffers or as party favors, the recipients will have to find their own ways to test them. By the way, I feel the need to warn you that "Reading this column will either make you pee your pants with laughter or put you to sleep."

33

What a Teal Deal!

It was five a.m. and there we were, picking our way by flashlight through an absolute maze of cattails that stood taller than me in a foot of slimy, oozy, stinking mud. I had never been here before, and my young guide had found our eventual destination only once before, during daylight. We were loaded to the hilt with shotguns and shells, camp stools, decoys and packs, and waddled along in chest waders, no less. So what could possibly go wrong?? Let me tell you.

Kansas has an early season in mid-September for a small duck called a Teal. My young guide Jared was also my young trapping apprentice who also happens to be an avid duck hunter. Convinced we could clobber a few teal for the table, even though more water dripped from my leaky bathtub faucet than was in the ponds around, we agreed to meet at the McPherson Valley Wetlands outside McPherson, Kansas. Jared had found a spot in the middle of the wetlands that still held a little water and suggested we meet at that early hour to beat the rush because everyone would be trying to find the best spots near what little water was left. I held my tongue but scoffed at the idea that anyone else would be silly enough to traipse through that swampy maze at five in the morning.

Just prior to five o'clock I turned down the gravel road toward the wetlands, quite prepared to have myself a nice nap while we awaited sunrise, but as I rounded the corner, my headlights fell upon pickup after pickup already parked. OK, my bad; so we weren't the only fruits in this basket!

We loaded ourselves with all the above-mentioned necessities and sallied forth. Down through the deep road ditch and up the other side, then picking our way along the top of a long dike, and finally down into the teeth of the oozy, stinking, sucking mud of the cattail swamp we trudged, shotgun slung over my shoulder, decoys and a camp stool in one hand, a flashlight in the other, and what had to be 50 pounds of shotgun shells in my vest pocket—and waddling in chest waders to boot. Don't get me wrong, chest waders are the bomb when you're in water up to your waist, but if you fall, it's like wearing a 50-gallon drum around each leg. It's easier to just fill them up the rest of the way and float away than to try to dump them out. But when they're sucking mud beneath your feet, chest waders are like wearing huge clown shoes. No matter how well they fit, you still walk like Flippo the Clown.

Back and forth and around through towering cattails we slogged. I was afraid we'd gone through a time warp somewhere and was prepared to be taken prisoner by Viet Cong soldiers anytime. Finally my young guide announced, "I think we're almost there." Awhile later, after he had proclaimed that for the fifth time, I told him "If you're talking about the backdoor to hell, we walked through that quite a ways back."

Finally we walked around a clump of cattails and into an opening, and there in front of us in the flashlight beam was a small pool of water. In the distance we could hear other hunters, obviously as cuckoo as we were. They spoke in muffled English, so I assumed they were not Viet Cong soldiers. Jared seemed to sense I was disgusted and struggling, so he pointed his flashlight beam to a clump of shorter cattails and told me "Put your camp stool there and get settled while I put out the decoys." Great, I thought. This should be a snap, shooting ducks from a comfortable camp stool.

The first problem soon appeared; there was not one dry centimeter anywhere to unload all my necessities while I set up my stool. My gear bag drew the short straw and was plopped into the mud as a workbench to hold my shotgun. I unfolded the little four-legged camp stool and began prospecting for a semi-level spot for all four legs, which was next to impossible, but I found it easily adjustable, as just a small amount of pressure on any leg pushed it slightly into the mud and leveled it out. Success!

With the camp stool set and leveled, I sucked each foot one at a time, out of the mire and slid my carcass into the seat. Now, it hadn't dawned on me that the same pressure that leveled each leg of the stool would now be multiplied by … let's just say a lot. The minute my butt hit the seat, the stool and I headed south for China. Sinking straight down would have been one thing, but both back stool legs suddenly became over-achievers and I was soon reclined backwards looking up at the stars. I squirmed and wiggled around and finally perfected some sort of move that rolled me out of the seat sideways onto all fours and into the muck. Around and around we went, that stool and I, until I somehow found that if I sat REAL still, we remained upright and stable. Bring on the teal, I thought!

As dawn finally spilled itself across the swamp and a few teal at a time graced us with flyovers, shotguns began to roar. My young guide harvested a few teal as the little beggars zoomed over us like fighter jets, and I found that the only thing worse than being old and slow was trying to shoot ducks from a camp stool in the mud. Every time I moved, whether to shoulder my shotgun or to scratch a body part, the stool threw a fit. I felt like I was on the kiddy ride at the fair, the one with the giant tea cups that bobble around as it turns.

Finally the ducks stopped flying, so we collected our gear and headed out. I told myself the trip out should be a snap since we could see where we were going. Wrong again; daylight made my gear no lighter, the muck no less "mucky" and the clown waders no easier to walk in.

As we picked our way back through the literal maze of skyscraper-high cattails, I became more amazed with every step that we had found this place in the utter blackness at five AM. The muck was outrageous. Just when I thought we were home free, the swamp monster beneath me grabbed both feet of my clown waders and wouldn't let go. I unfolded my camp stool and laid my shotgun on it to keep it out of the muck and away from the monster that held me captive.

Grabbing one leg of the boot with both hands, I began to extract it from the muck. Balance has never been my strong suit and, standing there with both feet mired fast in the muck and both hands on one leg, I began to wobble. Now, there was enough elastic in each shoulder strap that as I floundered about trying to retain my balance and my dignity, both feet pulled free from the boots and there I stood, upright with both boots stuck in the mire, but both feet standing inside the legs of my clown waders! So much for the dignity part!

Jared was stifling guffaws as I extracted myself, shouldered all my tackle and followed him on out of the quagmire. It's about teal season again, and he's promised me a nice dry teal hunt this year before he heads off to the marines in the fall. We'll see. I just hope that evening as he enjoyed his fresh teal dinner, he appreciated just how good I made him look that morning!

34

Xtreme Wildlife Rescue

Many people who feel called to "rescue" wildlife seem to lose all common sense somewhere along their journey. Now, I'm not talking about livestock that are part of a farmer's or rancher's living, which in most cases are treated way better than most wildlife, and sometimes better than some humans; in some cases, rightly so. Nor do I mean abandoned or mistreated dogs and cats that should be taken to shelters. I'm talkin' about perfectly healthy deer fawns, baby raccoons, owl chicks etc. that are found by well-meaning "wildlife heroes" and taken to animal rehab facilities instead of allowing Nature to reunite them with their parents the old fashioned way. Every year there are great-horned-owl chicks raised somewhere in our town park, and some years back, one of them ended up wedged behind a planter on a local family's porch. My wife and I "rescued" it and took it to a local rehab facility where we were mildly scolded and told to simply put it back in the park for its parents to find. When we turned him loose, "Ozzy" the owl flew half way across the park and was gone the next morning, just as the rehab people predicted.

My wife has gotten hooked on a couple British TV shows that are all about rescuing wildlife, and the British take that VERY seriously. Thing is, they rescue wildlife that don't need or really shouldn't be rescued. In one particular segment of the show they surgically repaired the broken leg of a robin; really? Now, I like robins as well as the next guy, but I'll bet the money spent on that operation could have bought real guns for a few of their "Bobbies" to carry instead of just nightsticks! If only they'd spend as much effort on finding a new phrase to replace "Bloody Hell!"

Then there are the snakes. Don't get me wrong, I'm a snake guy and have been known to ferry a certain huge bull snake with multiple eggs already in its throat from someone's henhouse to the river a couple miles away to be set free (but you didn't hear that from me.) On the TV shows self proclaimed heroes rescue huge boa constrictors and pythons that have evidently been turned loose by disenchanted owners who woke up one morning to find the beast wrapped around one of their body parts, prepping them as a snack. They bag them and take them back to their rehab center, where they weigh, measure and check them over to assure they are healthy. Even though snakes don't bother me, if I found a snake like that, the rescuers would find it to be very unhealthy when I delivered it. And then there's the question of what to do with them. Unless they plan to UPS them back to Africa where they belong, they can't just turn them loose in the neighbor's hayfield. I wonder if British homeless shelters accept snake meat.

The people on these shows act like their entrance into Heaven depends on the number of critters they snatch up (rescue.) One time they chased a pea hen (a female peacock) from rooftop to rooftop in a two-story apartment complex. I've had peacocks and they fly like 747 jumbo jets. If there had been a real farmer in the group, they would have known the thing would eventually simply fly back to where it came from!

Then there are the badgers. The British version of a badger looks slightly different than ours, and they don't seem to be as mean, but they're everywhere! Not an episode of the show goes by that they don't scoop up a badger from someone's flower garden. They have an entire commune of badgers back at their facility that will eventually be released back into the wild. If word ever got out that I caught and released a badger in these parts, I'd be the one needing rehab! And heaven forbid one of them should appear a little sickly; if so, it's all hands on deck and the animal ER springs into action! And if one of the little beggars happens to expire on their watch, it's Katie-bar-the-door and the whole staff appears to need grief counseling. I've come to wonder if they'll shed as many tears at their "mum's" passing.

A couple years back the North American Falconry Association (NAFA) held its annual convention in Hutchinson, Kansas. Amongst all the exotic birds of prey from all around the world sat Bob the Turkey Vulture. Now, Bob was regal in his own way, but sitting there on his

perch with his wings all fanned out, he looked like Goofy in a room full of Snow Whites.

Bob's story begins with falconers Mario and Brandi Nickerson from Ft. Worth, Texas, who also run Nature's Edge Wildlife Rescue, specializing in rescuing (there's that word again) reptiles and birds of prey. Some years back they got some calls about an errant buzzard in town, and one evening they were told the thing was waltzing around in the middle of the town football field while practice was in session. Can you imagine: to a football field full of city boys, that must have seemed like the stone gargoyle had come down from the front of the courthouse. The local animal control people were afraid to approach Bob, probably fearing he was Dracula in disguise and would pounce on them for a snack. When they arrived, Bob was on the roof of the house next door, so they retrieved a dead squirrel found stuck in the fence and tossed it near the house. Bob unceremoniously flew on down and began gnawing on their offering. With tarps, nets, an open pet crate at the ready and EMTs on standby, they surrounded ol' Bob, expecting a rodeo, but he again called their bluff and simply waddled into the crate with his snack in his mouth.

Back at the Nickerson's home, the crate containing Bob was put temporarily in their kitchen until they could figure out Bob's story. Maybe a vulture in your kitchen is the Texas equivalent of a garbage disposal? I'm thinkin' that to the British wildlife "rescuers," having a buzzard in your kitchen would put you right up there on a pedestal with the queen mum herself. Anyway, Brandi said that the next morning when the cage door was opened and she stood there with Bob's breakfast (one can only guess what that might have been) he aggressively charged out the door and across the kitchen for his handout. Long-story-short, they were pretty sure that, given Bob's reaction to humans and other physical characteristics they saw, he had been raised by humans and recently turned loose to fend for himself. I'm not sure what someone was thinking when they took in a turkey vulture chick as a pet. Did they not consider that one day it would grow into a full-grown buzzard? Would walking him through the park on a Sunday afternoon attract as many girls as a puppy? I suppose you could always fly him like a kite.

The Nickerson's credentials allow them to keep ol' Bob for educational purposes, which is good. I can only guess what goes through a first grader's mind when seeing a live turkey vulture close up. Although not really considered a pet, can you imagine the conversation starter Bob would be? And would you list him in your profile on an online dating site? "Outdoors-loving animal-rescue hero with pet turkey vulture looking for gal who likes black and has always wanted a pet buzzard in her kitchen." Anyway, I'm glad ol' Bob has found a good home, and who knows, maybe he can be trained to start the dishwasher and run the vacuum cleaner once in awhile!

35

You Don't Say!

My wife and I often pass the hours spent in a hunting blind by making up animal conversations for various situations. On a fall turkey hunt years ago, we had our hunting blind set up near an old feedlot. The owner had round bales stored there and a tractor path wound around through the bales. The turkeys followed the tractor path through the bales and into the pasture surrounding the old feedlot. We put a couple hen-turkey decoys just across the fence into the pasture and settled into our blind. The resident cattle soon came to see what was up and became enamored with the decoys. You could almost sense their thoughts, so we named the cows Clara, Elsie, Audrey and Bessie, and imagined their conversation something like this:

"They look like turkeys, but they sure don't move much," Clara said, staring at the decoys.

Elsie added, "Turkeys stink, but these things smell like tractor tires or something. Let's all run at them and see if they scatter and make those same funny noises turkeys make when we almost step on them."

Audrey weighed in, "No, I'm pretty sure they aren't real turkeys—if they were, they'd be eatin' corn out of our poo right now."

"Girls, I've got an idea," Bessie said, "Let's all back up and try to pee on them and see if they run like they usually do."

Perhaps the funniest animal conversation we ever conjured up came about at an old farmstead where we hunt deer. The abandoned farmyard sits back a long lane and we park our pickup there and walk to the nearby deer blind. We know deer routinely wander through the farmyard and around the old buildings, so we tried to imagine how they would react to our truck sitting there if they wandered through as we sat in the blind.

Here's the scene: One morning as we sit there in our deer blind, two deer, Bucky and Chloe stroll into the farmyard and come upon our pickup in the drive.

"See, Bucky," Chloe states, "I told you I smelled them again."

Bucky rests his chin on the hood of the pickup and replies "Yup, sure enough. Hood's still warm, they're here somewhere."

"What doofuses," Chloe retorts with disgust as she turns and begins to walk away. Meanwhile Bucky jumps up and sprawls out across the hood of the pickup with his front legs sticking out in front of him and his back legs out behind him, rolls his eyes back into his head and hangs his tongue out the side of his mouth.

Chloe hears the commotion, and just as she turns around, Bucky calls out "Ohhhhh Chloe, they got me!"

"You get off there this instant," Chloe scolds. "That's not funny at all anymore, especially after you got shot in the butt last season!"

The nursing/retirement home where I used to work has two dementia units and I often marveled at the strange things the residents there with dementia would say and think. Making up animal conversations may see pretty weird and even goofy, but I can only hope that filling my mind with silliness like that now will help me ramble on about silly stuff like that when I get dementia, rather than being mean and nasty and cussin' all the time!

36

You Just Might Be an Old Fisherman if...

It was the fishing trip from hell: I forgot to put the plug back into the drain hole in the transom and nearly sank the boat before I left the marina. After pumping out the boat, I pulled it over and tied up to the courtesy dock while I parked the truck and trailer. After firing up the motor and heading for open water, I looked back to discover I had forgotten to untie from the dock and had now towed it halfway across the lake. After sheepishly returning the AWOL dock, I again gunned the boat toward parts unknown, only to discover I had forgotten to fill the gas tank and was now adrift with the seagulls. It was time to admit I had finally become an old fisherman. As I awaited either help or a moment of clarity, I penned some thoughts that will help you decide for yourselves if you, too, might now be an old fisherman.

- You just might be an old fisherman if you still smell like Ben Gay even after you've cleaned your fish.

- If you waste countless hours of prime fishing time reeling and casting, reeling and casting, because you can't remember whether or not you just re-baited your hook, you might be an old fisherman.

- If, after reaching quickly under the boat seat for the dip net, you've found yourself holding your cane instead, you just might be an old fisherman.

- If you have ever started to hold the line between your teeth only to discover they're still at home on the night stand, you just might be an old fisherman.

- If your shore lunch now includes a tall, cool thermos of Metamucil and a box of prunes, you just might be an old fisherman.

- You just might be an old fisherman if you recently had to remove a seat from your boat to make room for your walker.

- You are probably an old fisherman if your reaction time has become so slow that fish congregate beneath your boat for the free meal, knowing they will never be hooked.

- If your fishing buddies are now more than happy to take you along to their secret "honey holes" because they are confident you'll never remember where you were anyway, you just might be an old fisherman.

- You just might be an old fisherman if your wife now begs to go fishing with you because she's afraid you'll forget your way back home.

- If removing that occasional fish bone from your teeth can now be accomplished by removing your teeth and tapping them on the table, you just might be an old fisherman.

- You are certainly an old fisherman if your glasses, hearing aids and dentures are now worth more than your pickup, boat and trailer.

- You just might be an old fisherman if your favorite fishing chair is now one of those fancy walkers with a seat on it, and you are relegated to fishing from the boat dock because that's the only place level enough to park it.

- You just might be an old fisherman if, to you, the letters GPS mean Gotta Pee Soon.

- You used to search garage sales for good used fishing gear, but if you now scour garage sales for containers that will make good emergency urinals for your boat because you have to pee so often, you are probably an old fisherman.

- It's easy for anyone to drive off with their coffee cup sitting on the roof or the bumper of the pickup, but if you have gotten to the lake and turned around to back your boat down the boat ramp only to discover it was still parked in the driveway at home, you just might be an old fisherman.

- And finally, you just might be an old fisherman if your eyesight has gotten so dim that you now haul home all the carp you catch because you mistake them for trophy bass.

www.ingramcontent.com/pod-product-compliance
Lightning Source LLC
Chambersburg PA
CBHW071405290426
44108CB00014B/1693